THIS FAR

THIS FAR

MY STORY OF LOVE, LOSS, AND EMBRACING THE LIGHT

ALLISON HOLKER

Harper Select

ISBN 978-1-4002-4894-0 (HC)
ISBN 978-1-4002-4897-1 (audiobook)
ISBN 978-1-4002-4895-7 (ePub)

Library of Congress Control Number: 2024948684

Printed in the United States of America
24 25 26 27 28 LBC 5 4 3 2 1

To my children—Weslie, Maddox, and Zaia—
whom I love beyond measure.
To my blood family and my chosen family, including
my team, who have supported me through it all.
And to my fans, who have given me angel wings.
I am so grateful.

The light shines in the darkness, and the darkness has not overcome it.

JOHN 1:5

Hope is being able to see that there is light despite all of the darkness.

DESMOND TUTU

The world breaks everyone and afterward many are strong at the broken places.

ERNEST HEMINGWAY, *A FAREWELL TO ARMS*

CONTENTS

PROLOGUE

A magical night in December. Stephen and I are driving, just the two of us, along the main strip in Laguna Beach, California, a picturesque place known for its coves and beaches and vibrant art scene. It's the perfect setting for this romantic interlude, a rare break from our responsibilities as parents and business partners.

The weekend getaway is Stephen's idea. We're celebrating our ninth wedding anniversary, and instead of settling for a one-night escape like in years past, he books us a room in a luxurious oceanside resort. To be fair, the only reason we end up in Laguna at all is because our daughter Weslie has a soccer game here. When Stephen suggests we check into a hotel Friday night, catch Weslie's game on Saturday, and take the rest of the weekend for ourselves, I don't hesitate. "Let's do it!" I tell him.

Since we got married in 2013, our lives have been amazingly, gratifyingly busy. Stephen and I are both workaholics who, through sheer will and an unshakable self-belief, have risen from modest beginnings to the top of the dance world. This year, 2022, has been especially hectic as we plant the seeds and toil in the field with the expectation of bountiful harvests in 2023 and 2024.

We met on Season 7 of the TV reality show *So You Think You Can Dance*, and our entire relationship has been wonderfully stuck in the honeymoon phase. Not long before Stephen schedules this romantic weekend, the teacher in Weslie's theology class asks all the students, "What's your favorite thing about this life?" Weslie's reply: "My parents' relationship. It is so beautiful. I want to have one like it someday."

Stephen and I are like music and dance, so conjoined it's hard to imagine either of us without the other. To emphasize that point, I write and produce (with the help of the internet) a beautiful song for him titled "Better Together," which covers our entire history together. It's my anniversary gift to him, and I play it for him while we are on our way to galleries to browse sculptures. I record his reaction. At first, he is annoyed at me for distracting him while he's driving, but as the song fills the car he goes from laughing to crying as quickly as a yellow light turns red.

Each verse summons a different memory, like how I went into labor with our son, Maddox, as an Easter party at our house was in full swing. Stephen has one hand on the wheel and his other hand is squeezing mine as he listens to the lyrics that repeat over and over how we're stronger together. Tears stream down his face, and he raises my hand to his lips to kiss it.

Stephen is not a natural crier. He has a resting smiley face. Seeing him so outwardly moved by my gift makes me deliriously happy. We have never seemed more in sync.

As if the universe is confirming our unwavering bond, at one of the next galleries we visit we stumble upon a romantic sculpture of two humans hugging and dancing. We buy the piece, agreeing that it beautifully embodies our connection. We are so stoked to imagine the sculpture enjoying pride of place in our home and then being passed on to our kids and their kids as a treasured heirloom.

The rest of the weekend passes in a beautiful blur. We talk a lot about the upcoming year. We are excited about the future and all the projects we have in the pipeline. Stephen has already shot an ad campaign for Gap Inc., and we are being offered two shows on major networks. We've collaborated on a children's book. I have a Barbie home makeover show for HGTV in the works.

We are actively engaged in growing our family, if you know what

I mean, and we do what it takes to conceive a child in Laguna. We're constantly talking about having more kids. In taking stock of our lives together, we feel truly blessed.

At the hotel, I open Stephen's anniversary gift to me. It is a gorgeous black Prada suit—a notable departure from the hoodie or cool kicks that I can count on from him.

Less than seventy-two hours later, Stephen is dead of a self-inflicted gunshot wound, and I'll spend the next year looking at that exquisite suit, our final weekend, and every single memory that preceded it through a different, distorted lens. Was he deceiving me during our time in Laguna? During our whole marriage? The storybook love that everybody said we had—was any of it real?

The questions are endless. Did he buy me a black Prada suit so I'd have a nice outfit to wear to his funeral? And if he did, was it one last gesture by an incurable romantic or just messed up beyond belief?

How long had he lived with the thought of killing himself?

Now when I watch the video I recorded of him in the car, Stephen's face is different from how I initially registered it. I look at his expression as he's listening to the song, and he's somewhere else. What made him believe that suicide was an appropriate response to whatever he was going through?

That Stephen would die by his own hand is incomprehensible to anyone who knew him. I'm completely blindsided. We are both people who spread positive energy, who are known for being joyful. Who are literally dancing through life. Stephen had never given me a reason to believe that he didn't appreciate the beauty of life, the gift of existing, as much as I do.

His suicide is an unnatural disaster, a megafire set by his hand that sweeps through our past, present, and future, reducing to ash every memory, plan, and dream that we shared. Stephen always saw himself as the protector of me and the kids—our Superman—and in the wake of his death I feel a duty to be his. So when possible clues emerge in his phone and his nightstand drawer and his shoeboxes for why he did what he did, my instinct is to keep them buried—as he had.

I want so much for him to be remembered as the beautiful light in the world that he was, even though his suicide casts our family into complete darkness. A total eclipse of the heart.

It is difficult to reconcile my feelings. I'm sad that Stephen would leave us this way because he was truly a good person, an incredible husband and father who positively influenced everyone with whom he came into contact. And yet, his actions are deeply traumatizing to me and our three children. Although I don't want him to be remembered for his final decision, I cannot ignore the impact it has had on our lives.

His unbearable pain becomes our family's collective cross to bear. My kids and I will never get over his death, and yet we must go forward. How do we manage that? Therapy is helpful. So, too, is dance. I'm not sure I fully appreciated until recently how dance has been the one constant for me in a life full of ups and downs. I've always been able to tell stories of love and loss and pain and exhilaration through movements of my body that heal and reveal.

It's common for the people left behind by suicide to wonder how they failed their loved ones. At first, I wallow in the what-ifs: *What signs did I miss? What could I have done better so that Stephen would still be here?* But then someone turns my perspective inside out by asking, "How long had Allison been carrying him through the darkness?" It's an interesting thought. Instead of focusing on what had gone wrong, what about all the things we had done right?

I'll never know, or understand, why Stephen decided to leave us. How his journey and mine inexplicably, irrevocably diverged. From *better together* to *forever apart* has been a vast—and harrowing—distance to bridge, but what choice have I had? I cannot—will not—let his decision define the rest of my life. I have come this far, with milestones and milestones still to go.

CHAPTER 1

RESOLVE AND RESILIENCE

I began life feeling self-consciously out of step, like I was marching to eight counts while everyone around me was keeping three-quarter time.

In my family I was the youngest of five children and the third girl, with four years separating me from my nearest sibling, my sister Becky. My parents used to joke that I was the child they didn't know they wanted. By the time I arrived in 1988, my parents were scrambling to make ends meet. They always seemed to be working, leaving me to be looked after by my two older brothers, whom I adored (and still do).

When they went off to college, I was largely on my own during my formative adolescent years. My four siblings had grown up navigating the peaks and valleys of childhood as a pack, but I was a soloist scaling that same sometimes treacherous terrain in much more precarious conditions.

The anxiety over money in our household when I was growing up permeated the walls like mold, triggering all kinds of reactions. My parents became phantom presences, my mom because she was holding down three jobs and my dad because he was chasing work overseas as a Mandarin translator for US-based companies. He'd spend upwards of six months at a time in Asia, mostly in China.

My siblings would fondly recount outings with Dad to the park or the skating rink as I sat in forlorn silence, racking my brain to recall a single time that he had taken me out to toss a ball or ride a bike. I craved time with my dad, an outgoing, charismatic storyteller who commands a room when he speaks. In my eyes, he was a larger-than-life presence whose patterned shirts and bright socks epitomized his colorful personality, and I yearned to be close to him.

The geographic distance between us during most of my teenage years, when I yearned for his presence the most, created an emotional divide that neither of us could bridge during his brief visits home. Yet I never doubted his immense love for me. And I definitely inherited from him my sense of adventure and my fearlessness to pursue my dreams and not be dissuaded by the obstacles thrown in my path, however daunting they were. I respect my dad for having a vision of a professional void he could fill in the Far East and going for it. I've looked to his inspiration in crafting my own work life, with one caveat: I want to carve out a better work-life balance. I want to be fearless and relentless in my career, but never at the expense of being present for my kids.

As much as I admire my dad's gumption, it doesn't change the fact that his absences created a kind of catch-22, because when he was home we had a difficult time bonding. We were like strangers who circled each other warily, unsure of what to say or how to act. I understood that he was doing the best he could to provide for us, but that didn't preclude me from struggling with feelings of abandonment. Daddy issues, I've heard them called.

From both my parents, but especially my mother, I learned the value of hard work, the power of perseverance, and the ability to take adversity and treat it like an adventure. She taught me that it didn't matter what job you held down, only that you performed it to the best of your abilities.

All you need to know about my mom is that she got a job in the stockroom at HomeGoods when she was in her *seventies*. By then, she had divorced my dad and was living in a house that I'd helped to provide for her. Her motivation for working had less to do with the paycheck than the sense of purpose the job provided. She said she needed something to do, somewhere to be, to fill her days. The long and unpredictable shifts and physical labor don't faze her. She's such a wonderful role model. I couldn't be prouder to be her daughter, but during my teenage years we had moments when our clashes severely tested our relationship.

When I was growing up, my mom worked out of absolute necessity. We would have been homeless if not for the money she brought in from her *three* jobs. Her day would start at five in the morning with her work at the factory where she meticulously crafted arrowheads for bows and arrows, labor that over time left her fingers gnarled with arthritis. From there, she'd put in an afternoon shift at Bath & Body Works and then report for her overnight shift restocking shelves at Nordstrom. I honestly don't know when, or if, she slept.

Try as they might, my parents never seemed to be able to ascend to a place of financial security. Anything new—clothing, furniture, electronics—was an extravagance. As my siblings moved on and out, I was left behind to navigate our increasingly complex family dynamics by myself. We were a large religious family, and yet I experienced an over-whelming sense of isolation. Despite my parents' best intentions, I grew up feeling insecure and unsafe.

There were months when we didn't have enough money to cover the rent. My parents never owned a home when I was growing up, and we moved frequently, downsizing as our financial circumstances dictated. I can vividly remember at least one instance when strangers came and repossessed our car, removing it right from the driveway to use as col-lateral after my dad, who was in Asia at the time, missed a payment to a loan shark. It largely fell on my mom to navigate the chaos and pick up the pieces—a role I would come to understand all too well.

My brothers, Dave and Aaron, both of whom were roughly a decade older than me, were my first heroes. I looked up to them so much. They both wrestled competitively, which meant that I wanted to wrestle when I grew up too. I'd steal their singlets and headgear and beg them to wrestle me, driving my prim mother to distraction. They didn't always mind me hanging around with them. They learned that I could be useful at the mall and the movie theaters, serving as catnip for the cute girls whose big sister–like fascination with me would lead to introductions to my brothers.

Inasmuch as I had a substitute father figure, Dave was it. I tagged along with him everywhere he went, including on one memorable trip to Las Vegas. We started out in St. George for a family party hosted by an aunt and just kept going another hour or two on I-15 to Vegas. Once inside a casino, Dave gave me strict orders to stay put while he went off to gamble. I did as I was told. But being so small, I must have stuck out, because pretty soon I was surrounded by cops who could clearly see I was too young to be on the gambling floor. They took me into their custody as a lost child until my brother could be tracked down and claim me. That was the end of that gambling adventure. We drove home. Our mom didn't know until years later about that little side trip, but we certainly had a good time, and we laugh so hard about it now.

Aaron was an amazing athlete. He became a three-time state champion in high school and represented Brigham Young University at the 1999 NCAA championships, finishing seventh in the 133-pound weight class. After BYU disbanded its wrestling program, he transferred to Iowa State and won the NCAA title in the 141-pound class in 2002 before embarking upon a career in the army as a logistics officer. I attended all my brothers' matches and whenever possible wore their discarded baggy clothes, again to the chagrin of my mother, who hand-sewed *Little House on the Prairie*–style dresses for my two sisters and me for Sunday church service. You can imagine my mother's relief when dance swooped in and delivered me from my rough-and-tumble tomboy ways.

I was nine or ten years old when dance tapped me on the shoulder with her magic wand and said, "I choose you." That's exactly how it felt: less like an act of free will on my part than a spell I fell under as I sat in the audience watching an international touring production that featured my sister Jessica, who was seven years older.

The performances mesmerized me. Until that moment, I had thought of dancers as dainty ballerinas twirling atop music boxes in tutus, sparkly tights, and uncomfortable pointe shoes. Angelic but aloof. Chilly. Remote. My seventeen-year-old sister and the older modern dancers prowling the stage were the opposite of that. They were powerful and athletic and fierce, warriors weaponizing their bodies to shatter the proverbial fourth wall. That flutter in your stomach when you first set eyes on your soul-mate? That's the feeling I got as I watched the dancers fly across the stage and stand strong in their power.

For the first, but not last, time, a circumstance nudged me toward genuinely embracing the New Age concept that whatever (and whom-ever) is meant for you will somehow find you. I knew instantly that dance was my destiny, which was wild because I was so old for a beginner. Most professionals have been dancing since they were toddlers. I didn't know what I didn't know, which turned out to be a blessing. My ignorance freed me from the self-consciousness and self-doubt that might have sunk my dream before it even shoved off from the dock to set sail.

I cannot adequately express how much dance has given me—how much it continues to give me. Dance is my foundation. It's my home base, my savior. It's still my gift, still my training, still my talent. Dance gave me both freedom and discipline.

Growing up, I was taught to see the world in black and white, but dance revealed to me all the beauty that exists in the gray areas in between. I think sometimes people get stuck in a binary mindset. Things are one thing or another: good or bad, right or wrong, strong or weak, a success or failure. I learned from dance to accept it all—the good, the bad, and the in-between.

I'm not sure what it says about my brain's wiring, but I like the con-fusion, the scariness of creativity. I love not knowing whether people are going to like what I created and then feeling reflected back to me whatever it is I've made people feel. Dance gave me that. I learned to appreciate all of it: the start, the process, the end. It's given me a lane, a safe path with which I've been able to experience a big life. When I work with younger dancers now, some of them are so talented—off-the-charts talented—but you can tell they're afraid of failing. So they don't extend themselves, don't see how high they could fly if they weren't so fearful of falling.

Maybe it was because of my late start, but I never cared about failing. Because I had so much catching up to do, I had the freedom to really, really try no matter the outcome. It helped enormously that it felt as if the dance steps were imprinted in my DNA. I didn't learn how to move my body; my body taught me how to move by tapping into the core of my being. The best way I can describe it is that I have an intuitive rhythm that makes it possible for me to connect to any piece of music. I've never looked at any dance style as something for which I need tons of formal training. I just let my body follow the music, and that organic movement provides the foundation for whatever dance I do.

It's not an overstatement to say that dance saved me. It gave me purpose, guidance, and direction at a time when my parents were pre-occupied and my siblings were off on their own big adventures. For better or worse, I was on my own, so I had no choice but to grow up fast. I'm not sure either of my parents knew what, or if, I ate all through high school. Neither was around during mealtimes to monitor my Hot Pockets consumption. Without the discipline and dedication that dance required of me, I could have stumbled down a terrible path.

In dance as in life, I followed the lead of my mom, who navigated challenging circumstances with unwavering determination. I adopted her mindset of "I have to do this on my own," which required pushing through, finding a way forward, and swallowing my complaints. That's how my mom rolled, and it became my guiding principle as well: Make the most of whatever you do.

Dance quickly became an integral part of my identity and purpose, and its community became my second home. It provided me with a safe haven beyond the reach of loan sharks or bill collectors. My instructors became guidance counselors, and the other dancers were like siblings with whom I shared a genuine bond.

I was so fortunate to end up at the Dance Club, a studio in Orem, Utah, owned and operated by Sheryl Dowling, who became like a surrogate mom to me. At the time, I saw her as a fancier version of my mom. They both were tiny framed but steely, with the same elegant grace and bob haircut. Like my mom, Sheryl encouraged my passion for dance. She believed in me. When I entered her dance studio, she made me feel seen and valued.

I studied contemporary, tap, ballet, and jazz, and by age twelve I found myself dancing alongside eighteen-year-olds on the premier dance team. I started out blithely believing that I was in control of my own destiny and that nothing could stop me. In fact, my path forward was really a tightrope with no safety net: One wrong step and my dreams could go splat.

Right before I hit my teenage years, my mom and I found ourselves in Sheryl's office. Reality had served me a devastating blow. "I can't dance anymore," I said through my tears.

The night before, my dad had delivered the gut-wrenching news: We simply couldn't afford my dancing. My sanctuary, my lighthouse of hope, was slipping from my grasp.

Sheryl was sympathetic. She nodded in understanding. Then, to my surprise, she extended me a lifeline. "I can offer you a job," she said.

Before she could finish the thought, my face lit up, and I said, "I'll take it! Whatever it is!"

Sheryl paid me generously, well beyond minimum wage, to serve as the studio's janitor. From the age of twelve until I graduated from high school at eighteen, I spent most evenings cleaning. My days were full. I'd go to school from early morning until 2:00, attend dance classes until 8:30, and then, after eating a quick dinner in the back room while finishing my homework, I'd spend the next few hours—sometimes until midnight—cleaning up after my fellow dancers. My mom, despite her workload, joined me whenever she could, and when my homework load was especially heavy, like in the lead-up to final exams, she'd take on all the studio cleaning herself.

The job allowed me to continue dancing, but it also, perhaps inevitably, altered my relationship with the other dancers. I was clearly marked as an "other," someone with fewer financial resources. Not that there hadn't been plenty of clues before. I wore clothes with holes and discarded leotards and leggings that I fished out of the lost-and-found bin. Since my mom was usually at work and my dad was gone, I relied on rides from my friends whose well-off parents chauffeured them to and from the studio.

Once I started my janitorial duties, some of the other dancers teased and taunted me. They left handprints on the mirrors, knowing I'd have to clean them later. They left cruel notes that said things like, "You're trash," knowing I'd find them while tidying up after them. There's a reason there are books written and movies made about mean girls. Teenage girls can be brutal, and the meanest ones at the studio zeroed in on me.

It was rough. Mopping floors, dusting trophies, vacuuming rooms, wiping down mirrors, scrubbing toilets, and cleaning the discarded food piles left by my peers while they returned to their comfortable lives was a humbling experience. As I collected and discarded other people's garbage, I sometimes did believe what those notes said: that I was also trash.

It could be an exhausting and lonely existence, but I had enough luminous moments to light my path. Renowned choreographers would occasionally visit, singling me out for praise and solo instruction, which made me feel special. They never ceased to be surprised to see me, the same dancer who had been featured in their routines, collecting garbage and preparing to scrub floors as everyone else packed up to leave. At the time, I was embarrassed that these important people saw me doing menial work. I wouldn't realize until much later that, far from putting them off, my work ethic made a positive impression on them.

I constantly worried about what others thought of me. I felt over-whelmingly ashamed and inferior. Resentment crept in. I looked around at the ease with which some of my classmates went about their days, and I wished for a life that wasn't so challenging. But deep down I knew I had no choice. I could pray for things to be different, but the reality was I had to put my head down and keep going.

What a gift it was to go through those hard times. I can see now that

I became stronger, more independent, more resilient, and more grateful for everything good that came my way.

Sheryl handed me the keys to the studio, placing complete trust in me when I was barely a teenager. I took that responsibility to heart. Never once did I fall short on the job. Never once did she have to reprimand me. I was there to study dance, but in the process I learned just as much about dedication, commitment, and an unshakable resolve to never give up.

My mother and Sheryl altered the course of my life—my mom by her example and Sheryl with her support. Reflecting on that challenging time, I am filled with gratitude. Despite the hardships, they envisioned a brighter future for me, and they got me to believe in that vision too.

To this day, I feel a considerable amount of pressure to succeed so that neither my mom nor Sheryl ever has a reason to feel that her support and sacrifices were wasted. Every opportunity feels like a duty I should take on because not only did I sacrifice my entire childhood to get to this position, but my mom made sacrifices of her own. She had an unfaltering faith in God that propelled her forward. And she gave me an unwavering belief in myself. I had talent, sure, and a work ethic. But I was lucky, too, to be in the right place at the right time.

Dancing on a team with older, more experienced kids accelerated my development. It was through my association with that group of teenagers that I got my baptism by fire—Earth, Wind & Fire, to be exact—at the closing ceremony of the 2002 Winter Olympics. They were held in Salt Lake City, a forty-five-minute drive from Orem. As first gigs go, it was incredibly memorable to share the stage with the genre-defying American band whose hit "September" would come to take on extra-special meaning in my married years.

I was fourteen years old—two years younger than the figure skater Sarah Hughes, who emerged as the youngest gold medalist of these Olympics. I had spent the weekends leading up to the Games immersed in rehearsals for the performance, so I was exquisitely trained. But nothing could have prepared me for the scene that greeted me outside Rice–Eccles Stadium the day of the closing ceremony. Figure skating legends Dorothy

Hamill, Scott Hamilton, and Katarina Witt were participating in the ceremony, and everywhere I looked it seemed as if there were some star, past or present, from the sports or musical worlds.

We were herded into tents that served as greenrooms while we waited to perform. I remember wandering off—maybe to use the restroom; my memory is foggy—and returning to a tent that contained a comfy couch. I sat down next to two guys wearing black-and-silver costumes with extravagantly painted faces. I complimented them on their makeup and their platform boots. "You look amazing," I said, truly meaning it. One of the guys jokingly asked me if I wanted to try on his boots. "Sure!" I replied with a laugh.

I had no clue who they were, but that didn't stop me from chatting with them for several minutes. I was so engrossed in the conversation that I was slow to pick up on the fact that no other young dancers were anywhere to be seen. "I must be in the wrong place!" I said brightly. I bounded off the couch and left my new friends behind.

I ran into them later, in the stadium tunnel leading to the stage, where people were screaming, "KISS! I love you!" And that's how I discovered the men I had been conversing with were members of the American rock band fronted by Gene Simmons. They performed "Rock and Roll All Nite" as I shook my head and thought to myself, *Oh my gosh! I was hanging out with KISS and I didn't even know it!*

The artistic director of the closing ceremony was Kenny Ortega, a legendary figure in the dance world who had worked with Cher, Rod Stewart, and KISS, among others. He had choreographed the iconic dance scene to "(I've Had) The Time of My Life" in *Dirty Dancing* and directed the 1993 movie *Hocus Pocus*, which I watched repeatedly as a child.

Two years after the Salt Lake City Olympics, Kenny would return to Utah to direct the movie *High School Musical*, and I would be cast as a cheerleader without having to audition. It was the first of a handful of acting credits I'd collect. I'd play an East High dancer in *High School*

Musical 2, a dancer on the TV show *House*, Gina in *Make Your Move*, and Devil Girl Charlie in the TV series *Hit the Floor*.

I wasn't the only performer plucked from the Olympics for *High School Musical*. Ryne Sanborn, who performed in the opening ceremony, would play a prominent role in the Disney movie that starred Zac Efron, Vanessa Hudgens, and Ashley Tisdale and premiered on January 20, 2006, roughly two weeks before I turned eighteen. We had the absolute best time during the filming. Hanging out with the cast, I experienced a richer social life than I did at my actual high school. In our downtime, I went bowling with the other actors or we descended on downtown Salt Lake City in a pack like typical teenagers, eating and laughing and gossiping and having a ball.

I'm not sure why I didn't have to audition. Maybe I was out of town. Around this time I started to travel extensively, my dance card filling up after I won Company Dance nationals in Florida and was named the National Senior Outstanding Dancer at the 2005 New York City Dance Alliance's national championship, held at Manhattan's Waldorf Astoria hotel.

The New York title was a big deal, the culmination of years of thirty-hour weeks spent in classes and rehearsals. With the title, which is more or less the dance equivalent of Miss Teen USA, came a one-year apprenticeship with New York City Dance Alliance conventions. I spent almost every weekend, from Friday through Sunday night, out of town, helping conduct classes and workshops and competitions. Saturdays and Sundays were reliably ten-to-twelve-hour days spent assisting teachers onstage, demonstrating steps if needed, or, if a teacher was absent, conducting the class myself. If the convention included a competition, I'd help facilitate getting dancers on and off the stage.

It was so much fun to meet up at these conventions with my other dancing friends from Massachusetts and West Virginia and other places far afield from Utah. No matter how busy we were, we always managed to find time to do something cool in whatever city we were in. We became a tight-knit family, and we pushed one another to become better dancers. It was the best training I could have asked for.

CHAPTER 2

DANCING FOR MY LIFE

I was straddling two worlds, adolescence and adulthood, and I wasn't always graceful in how I managed it. My last two years of high school, I was living very much like an independent adult. I was making good money working conventions during the weekends while juggling my course load. I was almost completely self-sufficient. I'd get myself to the airport on Fridays—a one-hour commute each way—and return to Utah Sunday night or early Monday morning. Sometimes I had to head directly to school when I got back.

The weekends I was in New York, I'd sometimes be out until the wee hours on the final night, hopping on and off the subway cars to find the cheapest, most delicious slices of pizza or the best street vendor hot dog or the hottest clubs where kids our age could hang out. Can I tell you how much I loved navigating the subways and buses in Manhattan as an out-of-town teen? I was like an older version of Madeline, minus the hat and hair bow, spilling out of the Waldorf Astoria to happily wander the city at all hours.

The first time I took the subway by myself, I was fifteen or sixteen years old, this tiny, sub-five-foot human fresh off the plane from Utah. I was lugging two suitcases on wheels and had printouts of the subway lines I needed to take to arrive where I was staying in Harlem. I remember being daunted by the prospect of carrying myself and those two sizable suitcases down multiple series of stairs to the subway platform. But I couldn't afford to take a taxi, so problem-solving on the run, I carried one suitcase down each set of steps, returned to retrieve the other one, and kept up this one-person relay until I could flag down someone to show me how to buy a token, which had not yet been replaced by a MetroCard. That first ride from Times Square to somewhere around 132nd Street and Broadway, if my memory serves, was harrowing. There were so many people and so many stops that I nearly had a panic attack because I talked myself into thinking that I must have gone too far.

Every trip to New York resulted in fresh tales of hilarity. One time a bunch of us staying at the Waldorf Astoria decided it would be fun to hang out on the rooftop, even though it meant climbing through a window to access it. Clearly, the lack of direct means of entry indicated that it was not someplace we were supposed to go, but we were undeterred. Six or seven of us were in an elevator ascending to the top floors when it stopped. We stood there, suspended between floors, for at least a half hour. I was such a rule follower that I was in a total panic. I wasn't sure we should pick up the emergency phone and ask for help since we technically had no valid reason to be there. If we were freed, I was worried we'd be going straight to jail. I was never so happy to see an ax-head bust through the doors. And no, we weren't busted by security.

I managed to get myself out of innumerable jams, always in time to catch whatever early-morning flight I was booked on to make it back in time for school on Monday. Plenty of times I was running frightfully late to get to my boarding gate and had to lean on my ingenuity to make my flight. As one might expect of a dancer, I was quick on my feet. If the line to clear security was long, I'd shout, "Mom!" Dozens of women's heads would reflexively turn toward the sound of my voice, and after they turned back around, I'd slip between two of the moms nearest to the front and closest to each other, so each would assume I was the offspring of the other.

Speaking of Mom, I brought mine home a light pink Kate Spade knockoff purse that I had bought from a street vendor. It looked so real she never knew the difference.

I felt so grown-up negotiating the multitudes of people and predicaments I encountered during my travels, so you can imagine my chagrin when my mom gave me a nonnegotiable ten o'clock curfew at home. We were at odds often during this time. It was confusing to experience so much independence on the road only to return home and be treated like a child.

My senior year in high school, I took a mythology course I absolutely loved. To this day, I think there's something so magical about the stories of the Greek gods and the life lessons embedded in them. I went above and beyond on the assignments—that's a fact. But it's also true that I missed classes on Fridays and some Mondays because of my work with the dance conventions. I had permission from school officials not to attend class as long as I turned in my assignments and kept up my grades, which I did.

One Monday, I traveled straight from the airport to school and showed up late to my mythology class. I walked in holding a project that was due, but the teacher extended me no grace. In front of the other twenty-nine students, she upbraided me. "What are you doing?" I remember her saying. "Dancing is a waste of time. You're wasting your time. You could be doing so much more. You could go to college . . ."

I was so taken aback, my response flew out of my mouth before my brain could stop it. I'm not proud of what I said, but I returned her rudeness in kind. "What do you mean I'm wasting my time?" I replied. "I'm making more money than you." Hands down, it's one of the cruelest things I've ever said to anybody.

As you can imagine, it was not well received. I was sent to the principal's office, and my mom was summoned. She showed up, and while she was understandably upset that I would say something so brutal to an authority figure, she stuck up for me.

"Well, she's not wrong," she said, before pointedly asking the principal why any teacher would belittle a student in front of the class like that, especially given that the student was clearly so passionate about the activity in question. While ashamed of what I said—it makes me blush even putting it down on the page—I was proud to have a mom who wondered if the teacher was right but was willing to defend me anyway.

My mom's support meant even more considering I had deeply, deeply wounded her the prior year by rejecting her religion, which is to her what dance became for me: a refuge and reason for being.

Throughout much of my early life, I was an active participant in the church. I saw religion as a source of beauty and wonder. But as I settled into my teenage years, I began to feel disconnected from some of the religion's teachings. And each time I posed a question, instead of receiving answers I was reprimanded for my curiosity and steered toward more stringent lessons and extended studying hours.

When I was sixteen years old, the incongruities and contradictions between some of the teachings and my beliefs became too much for me to reconcile. My questions became more pointed, and my skepticism resulted in my being sent to a church elder to shore up my faith. I had to read Scripture aloud to him every Sunday after church, but instead of clarifying the teachings, all that reading only made me question more things. And no matter what I asked, no one in a position of authority ever seemed able to supply an answer.

As a high school junior, I arrived at the decision to distance myself from the religion because it no longer resonated with my own beliefs. Despite my deep and abiding affection for the individuals within the church, I didn't experience an internal connection to the faith.

My decision to leave my family's church had long-ranging ramifications. It became a major source of sorrow for my parents, who were heartbroken. Our interactions devolved into intense arguments and heated discussions. At one point, I even moved out of the house to live with a friend's family. My mom, especially, had a hard time seeing that my actions weren't rooted in rebellion. I wasn't aiming to hurt anybody; I was following my convictions and striving to be true to myself.

While I had anticipated the impact leaving the church might have on my home life, I was in no way prepared for the reaction I received at school. Overnight, long-standing ties were severed. Friends stopped associating with me, spurred on by their parents, who said I was a terrible influence even though I didn't smoke or drink, worked hard, and made good grades. I had been nominated to become the captain of the school's dance team, and it appeared that I was running uncontested, as no other names appeared on the original list. My captaincy did seem a foregone conclusion, given what I had already accomplished as a dancer and choreographer. However, the day the nominations were unveiled, I was shocked to find my name replaced by others.

Perplexed, I approached the dance team coach, seeking an explanation. In an interesting twist, she also was a student in an adult class I taught at Sheryl's studio. She was blunt in her response: "I don't believe you set a good example for the girls. Your shift away from attending church concerns me. To be considered for a nomination, you'll need to resume attending church."

Excuse me? I was caught off guard, especially considering we were at a *public* school. Seeking guidance, I approached some of my other teachers to assess whether this discriminatory treatment was permissible or even legal. They rallied to my defense and brought the issue to the principal's attention.

My mom, despite her absolute heartbreak over my decision to leave the religion, also advocated for me. I felt so loved by her showing up like she did. She attended meetings at the school because she and my dad recognized what the coach had done was unjust.

At the end of the day, the principal sided with my coach, and I made the difficult decision to step away from the school's dance team for my senior year. Instead of choreographing routines and spreading school spirit, I auditioned for, and made, a career-changing appearance on the TV reality show *So You Think You Can Dance*.

All these years later, my photo is on the wall of fame at the school. As they say, God works in mysterious ways.

It is still baffling to me that I could be treated like a terrible disappointment when I was a straight-A student who devoted significant time to dance and worked a full-time job. It seemed as if I could do nothing right. I was subjected to cruel gossip and harsh judgment at school and at the dance studio, both places that I had counted on for stability. Was that because of my religious beliefs? Or was jealousy stemming from my early success in dancing at play? When I started wearing crop tops to dance rehearsals because I wanted to dress like the professionals I admired, the other parents loudly voiced their disapproval. They portrayed me as some kind of troublemaker hell-bent on leading all their dear daughters to dress provocatively. But was it moral outrage they felt, or was my talent in some way threatening to them? Whatever the reason, the studio became less of a refuge, even as dancing remained my sanctuary. It was my saving grace, offering me the space to channel my emotions through movement.

When I look back at this time in my life, I see my decision to leave the church as a character-building act that was pivotal in creating the person I'd become. It was an act of bravery to fight for my beliefs, and it set me on a course of self-discovery. It forced me to seek out my own community, my own people, and actively question the status quo. To search for answers instead of blindly accepting what I should think. The experience made me more comfortable being an outsider, an oddball. I think it's why I'm able to make people feel safe with their own opinions, even if I don't share them.

I have nothing but love and respect for the people I sparred with over my decision. The religion I left instilled in me my morals, my family values, my sense of commitment and loyalty. It gave me so much for which I'll be everlastingly grateful. Yes, leaving the religion resulted in my being viewed as a negative influence, a "problem child," by some people. But those same people contributed to making me the person I am today. I grew more comfortable with uncertainty. I learned that I didn't mind questioning the universe. I realized it's okay not to have every answer— and that I don't have to be so scared of not knowing something that I double down on the status quo. But all of this self-knowledge was hard-won. I didn't acquire it overnight. In the beginning, I internalized the things I was being told. I believed that I was a terrible person and that God hated me.

And then, at seventeen, I had an experience so traumatizing that it seemed to confirm in my own mind the worst that people were saying about me. I won't share specifics, but the fallout touched every part of my life.

Initially I kept what happened a secret. There was an incriminating little voice inside my head telling me that it was my punishment from God for having turned my back on my religion—which I now can see was a terrible insult to God. When my parents finally learned what happened, they were angry: with the person who had harmed me, with themselves for not keeping me safe, and even with me, for seemingly bringing this on with my act of rebellion. I think part of me knew that wasn't true; I wasn't the one who had done anything wrong. But for a long time I blamed myself and was burdened with shame.

I convinced my parents not to say or do anything and did what I could to put the incident behind me. In retrospect, I wish I had taken action. I have so much sympathy and compassion for those in similar situations who are too scared to speak out. I hope by giving voice to my regrets, I motivate others to stand up for themselves. Do as I say and not as I did.

What I went through drove home the lesson that life is inherently messy. It's inevitable that we will all grapple with pain, chaos, and uncertainty, and that's okay because those experiences are what foster our growth and learning. Those experiences don't define us; what defines us is how we navigate them. One of the most challenging aspects of life is believing in the light when darkness is all around us. It's essential to hold on to hope and trust that better times are just around the corner.

Thank God I had such a beautiful outlet to express my trauma. Despite moving forward as best I could, what happened absolutely informed my dancing over the years. Much, much later, during my All-Star season on *So You Think You Can Dance*, Sonya Tayeh choreographed a routine for me that told the story of someone being terribly mistreated—not in the same way that I was, but still, I was able to use the performance to energetically and therapeutically let go of the trauma and pain. Dancing through it was my way to bring to the surface long-buried memories and emotions and purge them. I feel like that performance was a big release, allowing me to dispel a traumatic experience that had been festering like a poison inside me.

As a dancer, I've embraced dark roles—welcomed them, even, because they allow me to tap into my own past experiences, even if they aren't exactly what I'm portraying—and shed heavy emotions and distressing memories. Luckily for me, my coming of age as a dancer coincided with the creation of a TV franchise that swept dancers out of the background, where they had long resided, and into the spotlight.

CHAPTER 3

SO YOU THINK YOU CAN DANCE

G rowing up, I was convinced, contrary to all reason, that dance would be my career. I didn't know how, I couldn't articulate why, but I knew in my heart of hearts that I was going to become incredible at dance and be hugely successful. I never doubted that everything would work out. My mythology teacher wasn't the only one who considered me delusional. My father hadn't seen me perform onstage since I was twelve, having assumed dance was a childhood passion that I'd eventually shed along with my braces.

I didn't need his approval (though I would later get it). All you have to do is find your people, and they don't have to be your family of origin. It's amazing how high and far you can fly when you are surrounded by a supportive flock all pointed in the same direction. I'm fortunate to have had the same core group of friends since I was sixteen—all dancers—most of whom I became close to while working the conventions. Everyone shared the same dream about becoming a big success, and I have to give it up to us because we all made it. I don't hold a grudge against the people who thought my friends and I were seriously misguided. I'm not so blind that I couldn't see where the naysayers were coming from.

Talents like Gregory Hines in tap and Mikhail Baryshnikov in ballet gave dancers cachet, but they were neither of my generation nor, you know, women. I admired them but I couldn't relate to them. Michael Jackson invoked the Holy Spirit with every step, but his songs were what made him the biggest pop star of the 1980s. Debbie Allen was a beautiful dancer and first-rate choreographer who imbued a love for dance in countless kids through her eponymous studios, but the public knew her primarily for her acting and directing. Madonna and Paula Abdul were dancers, first and foremost, but they became famous for their singing. I had to go all the way back to my grandparents' generation to find one of my enduring dance idols, Cyd Charisse, who appeared alongside Gene Kelly in multiple musicals in the 1950s, including 1952's *Singin' in the Rain*.

The timing of my breakthrough as a dancer couldn't have been luckier. I won the National Senior Outstanding Dancer title—in a bargain-basement black dress with spaghetti straps that my mother bought me so that I would wear it and feel her metaphorically hugging me since she couldn't make the trip—the same summer that *Dancing with the Stars* made its debut on ABC and *So You Think You Can Dance* premiered on Fox. The audience that I performed in front of en route to that title included producers and directors of Broadway shows but also choreographers who would be employed by those two shows. So they knew me (and in some cases, I had worked alongside them at conventions) long before I debuted on *SYTYCD*.

I was not an unknown entity to the show's regulars, and the public was developing a vocabulary, a sophistication, to understand what dancers did, which hadn't been the case before the shows aired. All of a sudden, the general public was dissecting such nuances as the carriage of a dancer's rib cage. *SYTYCD* became a game changer, with millions of rabid viewers. But I had no idea that any of that would come to pass when I auditioned—and neither did anyone I told about this little TV show I was trying out for.

SYTYCD was not a game changer because it introduced dance to the public. If you think about it, dance is like love. It's all around us if you're paying attention. Musicals have been winning awards for years and years, and not just because of the quality of the singing. The first musical to win the Academy Award for Best Picture was *The Broadway Melody* in 1929. The 1994 animated feature film *The Lion King* features hip-hop, jazz, modern, African, Caribbean, and ballet. People don't always make the connection, but the feelings and emotions of the characters are conveyed through their movements.

Consider the award shows you find particularly entertaining, the commercials that stick in your mind. Chances are they include dancing. How memorable would a wedding be if there was no dancing? How fun would a prom be without dancing? If you look back at some of the most beautiful moments of your life, the times when you felt the deepest connection to somebody, dancing often was involved.

Neither was *SYTYCD* a game changer because it gave people permission to dance. If you hear music, you almost can't help but move to the beat. I reject outright the notion that anybody is born with two left feet. To those who say that, I would say this: Dance is nothing more than walking with style and grace. Everyone has a dancer inside them looking for any opportunity to break out. Did you just turn your head? That's a dance move. Shuffle your feet? Dance move. Stretch an arm skyward? Dance move. Grab something? Dance move. Spin around? Dance move.

Can you take four steps forward, look over your left shoulder, look over your right shoulder, and reach for the sky with your left arm? Great! You're dancing. Granted, once you add music, it becomes a little harder to move to the tempo, but that can be taught. The moves themselves are second nature.

The mark that *So You Think You Can Dance*—and *Dancing with the Stars*—made on the world, and our industry, is that they showed people the craft behind the locomotion. The viewing public gained an appreciation for an art form that it might not have ever considered or cared about.

Both shows took dancers, who traditionally operated in the shadows of the more acclaimed singer or actor as storyteller, and made them the focal point through documentary-style storytelling. They demonstrated beyond a shadow of a doubt that dancers are also capable of telling stories using their bodies instead of their voices, narratives that can reach right down into your soul and shake it awake.

Dance was presented as a beautiful art form and not just a backup act. The magic of *SYTYCD* is it showcases dancers as storytellers. When I listen to a trumpet player, I don't know what note they're hitting, but I can clearly recognize the note took me somewhere emotionally. It's the same thing with dancers. You may not know what steps we're doing, but using our bodies as our instruments, we can take you somewhere emotionally.

My greatest gift as a dancer is my ability to tap into memories, to channel big and little emotions that I've kept bottled up inside, to make you feel something. I'm not the best dancer you'll ever see. I'll never be the best technician. But I might be the best storyteller. Using my body, I can make you believe, for example, that I'm a wife cowering in the kitchen as her mean drunkard of a husband bursts through the front door. I can make you think of your mother's final moments and the last breath she took with you in the room. I can transport you to that moment when you decided to leave the person who was physically abusing you, took that first step, and have never looked back. I can take you back to the first dance you shared with your partner at your wedding and help you access deep, romantic, beautiful, joyful moments—without opening my mouth.

And if I'm honest, *SYTYCD* (and *DWTS*) opened the public's eyes to the fact that dance does not begin with tap and end with ballet. Both shows did a great job of exposing viewers to all different styles—Latin, ballroom, hip-hop, jazz, and contemporary—so that when people heard the word *dance* they didn't automatically think of ballet.

I tried out for *SYTYCD* on a lark. Sheryl had a daughter, Jackie, who lived in New York City and was a Radio City Rockette. A decade older than me, Jackie was *amazing*, and I looked up to her (and not just figuratively; she was six feet tall without shoes). She attended an open-call audition for *SYTYCD* in the city and advanced out of the first round, but because of her generosity of spirit, her tryout ended up changing *my* life. Instead of holding on to the glory for herself, she called her mom and told her that I should audition for the show. She suspected the judges would consider my talent, in concert with my outgoing personality, an irresistible combination. If nothing else, she said, going through the audition process would be a good experience for me.

Since I hadn't watched the first season, I typed "So You Think You Can Dance" into a search engine, found out there were upcoming auditions in Los Angeles at the Orpheum Theater, and arranged to attend them. I had just gotten my braces off, so you know I was feeling myself. My mom volunteered to drive me to Los Angeles, a ten-hour drive each way. I was so thrilled to be there. I danced my heart out for my solo and had a blast. The judges, including Nigel Lythgoe, Brian Friedman, and Mary Murphy, advanced me to the next round.

I was so excited I ran off the stage and bolted from the theater like a football receiver running straight out of the end zone and through the tunnel after scoring a touchdown. The show's producers chased me down and hurriedly called me back. They needed me to dance again because they didn't have the musical rights to the original song I had selected. I had to improvise a whole new solo to a different song, which was no problem for me since I can move my body to just about any rhythm.

The fact that I had already secured a spot in the next round took all the pressure off, allowing me to enjoy the performance. I was so proud of myself and so excited to have crushed my first audition. It bolstered my self-belief and made me feel like, *I can do this*. I already had proof that I was on the right track. To then be handed a golden ticket straight to Las Vegas, allowing me to advance directly to the final round of qualifying, was beyond my wildest expectations. I was thrilled.

I also had no idea what to expect. It's not as if I'd grown up aspiring to be on TV or a soloist. Dancers at the time tended to be viewed as interchangeable, and I wasn't immune to that thinking. My goal was to be just like my sister Jessica, who was heavily involved in the theater scene and had a long-running gig in the Celine Dion show in Las Vegas before joining Cirque du Soleil. She was, and continues to be, a huge inspiration, and I can never repay her for all she has done for me. When I found out the winner of *SYTYCD* earned a one-year contract to appear in Celine's show, I burst into tears. It had been a pie-in-the-sky dream of mine to dance professionally alongside my sister, and now there was a chance that could happen.

I stuck around in LA to watch the other auditions, and I saw many talented friends get eliminated, one after the other. It made me appreciate the intensity of the competition I had somehow managed to survive. These were some of the best dancers I knew, and for them not to advance to the next round made me more nervous. So much for that victory lap. Despite having made it through, I recognized that I had to elevate my skills. I could not afford to become complacent.

I returned to Utah with a newfound motivation to train and improve before the upcoming Vegas qualifying, which was a couple of months away. Back at home, I found myself on stage with the renowned choreographer and teacher AC Ciulla in front of a crowd of about three hundred dancers. I was demonstrating movements without music, just counting my steps, when one of my legs went rubbery and I took a hard fall. Everyone in the room heard a loud snapping sound. I had torn my left meniscus. My entire body was flooded with pain and fear. Sheryl was there, and she rushed to the stage while the choreographer continued counting, oblivious to my distress.

I was gingerly transported to the hospital and, thanks to Sheryl's connections, was able to promptly get seen by a surgeon who recommended surgery. At that moment, I thought my chances of competing on *SYTYCD* were shattered. I was facing a three-month recovery period for a meniscus tear, and I was supposed to be in Vegas in less than two months. I was deflated but not defeated. I had gotten this far, and I wasn't going to give up without a fight. I rested briefly and then dove into physical therapy.

I was terribly nervous when I arrived in Las Vegas. The production team inquired about injuries, and I chose not to disclose mine, sensing they'd see me as damaged goods and cut me without giving me the chance to perform. This was the season that they introduced a scoring system for various rounds—jazz, hip-hop, ballroom, choreography, and solo—and a score of six or seven out of ten meant potential elimination unless you were able to save your spot with a sparkling solo. Throughout the rounds, I received one nine and all the rest tens.

Travis Wall, my best friend dating back to our convention days, received similar scores. Out of 116 dancers, we made the top twenty. Travis and I emerged as the highest-scoring male and female contestants. (We would go on to be nominated for a handful of Emmys between us, and Travis would notch multiple wins.) The only thing better than being on top is making it there alongside a longtime confidant.

Leaving Las Vegas, Travis and I knew we had secured spots on the show. However, we now had to submit to psychological tests, physicals, and other assessments, which meant I had to continue keeping my recent surgery a secret. Keeping the information under wraps wasn't as hard as it might sound. Injuries are an occupational hazard in dancing. The longer you dance, the more companionable your relationship to pain becomes. Over the years I've had to push through all kinds of aches and pains, smiling all the while. Broken toes, cracked ribs, a fractured collarbone, sprained ankles: You name it, I've danced through it.

As a performer, I've been trained to put on a good show even when I'm in extreme physical discomfort. Years later, I'd unfortunately see that this skill set—the ability to perform while hurting and never show it—could carry over to everyday life.

On the show, I was paired with Ivan Koumaev, a hip-hop dancer from Seattle and an absolute sweetheart. To this day, he remains one of my good friends. He's incredibly lovely, and I felt fortunate to have him as a partner. Ivan has a playful personality and is so much fun to be around. He brought an infectious spirit to our performances. Each week we drew a dance style from a hat, not knowing if we'd pull one that we had experience with or who the choreographer would be. Our first dance was a salsa, and it was hilariously bad. Ivan wore this pink hat that distracted the judges. Despite being praised for the dance, we knew our performance wasn't going to cut it. We needed to improve, and fast.

Win or lose, Ivan and I had a blast. I was only eighteen, the minimum age to compete—and viewers got to witness my metamorphosis from a child to a woman as the season progressed. It's not a coincidence that the dance of ours that seemed to stick in people's memories was to the Annie Lennox song "Why." I was the youngest competitor that season, the baby, but that dance was choreographed to show my transformation from a bubbly girl to a mature woman. It wasn't a difficult leap for me; I was growing so much as a person and a performer. I absorbed everything I could from the LA culture. I was around so many dancing legends whose expertise I soaked up like a sponge. Life will present you with opportunities, and if you're ready to seize them, that's when the magic happens.

The funny thing is, the week before my breakout performance to "Why," our West Coast swing routine made VH1's top-ten worst list. Because the stakes seemed relatively low—none of us had any expectations of becoming rich or famous—my attitude was *You can love me or laugh at me, and either way I'll be perfectly fine*. We weren't focused on the substantial audience the show was building, an audience eager to embrace us and inclined to view us more as distinct individuals than the faceless performers dancers historically had been.

There was a different energy in those first few seasons. What made the show so gritty and real, what attracted such a devoted following, was the guilelessness of the contestants. We literally were the boys and girls next door. No one had any expectations that the show could be a springboard to red-carpet appearances or bigger jobs (although the yearlong contract with Dion's Las Vegas show certainly was enticing). At the end of the day, we were drawn to the show by our passion for the craft. We needed our next dance like we needed our next breath. That purity of purpose, I think, is what struck a chord with the audience.

The prospect of working with some of the best choreographers was its own reward. As I said, many of them were already known to me. They were all the best in the field, and my goal was to learn as much as I could and have a great experience. A fringe benefit of being on the show was getting the opportunity to connect with people from diverse backgrounds. Growing up in a town where everyone looked like me, I found it eye-opening to encounter people who didn't share my background or religion and weren't judging me for my differences. I found the diversity liberating. It was a facet of my early success that I truly cherished.

The public was part of the voting each week, and I was propelled along by young women my age who saw shades of themselves in me—and their mothers who related to me as someone's daughter. I remember talking to one teenage fan after the season who told me that she threw a shoe at the television when I was voted off, prompting her to get grounded by her parents. That was certainly unexpected!

What surprised me the most was the support I received from dads. They seemed to connect to me, not in a creepy, predatory way but in the most wholesome way imaginable. It was as if I served as a kind of human bridge that helped them connect with the music and dancing of their daughters. I heard from so many men who said my routines changed the way they thought about dance, because the truth was they hadn't really thought about it at all before.

And who knows? Perhaps fathers saw me as a symbol of sorts of their own big-dreaming daughters.

The "girl dad" support that meant the most to me came from my own father, who was in the studio audience alongside the rest of my family one week. Looking out and locking eyes with him and my mother and sisters and brothers was one of the most magical moments of my life. I remember thinking to myself that I must be doing something right for all of them to be present and cheering me on. It was a rare moment; there simply hadn't been many times in my childhood when everyone was able to physically come together to support me, so for them to have made the effort created an indelible memory.

I finished in the top eight, which I thought was great. The week I was voted off the show, we were asked to prepare two solos. I had chosen "Feeling Good" by Michael Bublé and "This Woman's Work" by Kate

Bush. Walking down the hallway that morning, I encountered Mary Murphy, who was usually so warm and lovely. On this day, she could barely make eye contact with me. That's how I knew my time on the show was up. Mary's energy telegraphed my fate. In a panic, I approached a producer at the last minute and requested to switch my solo songs. Thankfully, I was able to. Can you imagine being eliminated and then having to dance to "Feeling Good"?! No thank you!

The competitor in me was bummed to be done, but my disappointment was overshadowed by the immense gratitude I felt to have shared a space, and such an amazing experience, with the other contestants and the choreographers and everyone else involved with the show. As a way of expressing my appreciation, I was determined to stay present and perform my best to the very end. If I was leaving, I was going to give it my all until the final note. Travis and I hadn't gotten to dance together on the show, and so many people wanted to see it. I hurriedly informed Travis that I was pretty sure I was being voted off. It was now or never. At the end of the show during the elimination segment, when my name was announced, I suggested that he step forward so we could dance an improvised routine together. He couldn't believe my time on the show was ending. He was sure I was mistaken.

When my name was called, Travis stepped forward, as we had planned, but he was so emotional that he couldn't move. It broke him that I was going home, and he froze. He just stood there with tears in his eyes as I danced around him. It turns out there was one thing worse than getting voted off the show, and that was seeing your longtime best friend visibly moved to tears by your elimination. The tears would be replaced by laughter—so much laughter—after the final show when Travis and I were part of the postseason dance tour.

A *dance* tour! What were we, rock stars? It was wild. I had gone to London to perform my routine after my National Senior Outstanding Dancer title, and I thought *that* was grand, but the tour arranged by the show was something even more awe-inspiring. At every stop we'd perform a couple of shows in front of audience members who had our faces plastered on their T-shirts. *What is happening here?* We'd look at each other in wonder. The first time I saw someone wearing my face, I literally asked the woman for the shirt off her back. I went back to my dressing room and got her a T-shirt from the show, and we swapped tops.

Around this time I sat for my first interview with a weekly tabloid devoted to celebrity stories and sightings. What place did I have in its pages? I was speechless. One of the questions I was asked is if I had a boyfriend. As a matter of fact, I did. I offered his initials: J. T. I didn't think twice about it, but once the issue came out, friends back home read that and went wild. "Oh man," they said, "did you read where Allison is dating Justin Timberlake?" (Let the record show that I was *not* dating *that* J. T.!)

In any event, we never knew we could be dancers and be celebrated like we were.

In addition to the pay we received for being part of the tour, we also received a weekly allowance of more than five hundred dollars for meals and other essentials. Did I eat well? Or save a lot? No and no. I survived mostly on pizza slices and street vendor hot dogs and spent most of my money on random stuff. Clothes, shoes, and Blockbuster runs for DVDs of all my favorite movies: *Singin' in the Rain, An American in Paris, West Side Story, The Red Shoes, Meet Me in Las Vegas.* Sorry, not sorry. I was eighteen and living my best life. At every stop, I made sure we'd make a visit to a big landmark and/or book a massage and/or eat one decent meal. Everywhere we went, we stayed at nice hotels, though it wouldn't have mattered because I honestly can't remember sleeping much. We each had our own rooms, but that didn't keep us from bunking four to a room so we could hang out together until one by one we all fell asleep.

Travis and I were always the last to nod off, so we'd grab pillows and a blanket and retreat to the bathtub, so as not to disturb anybody, and binge-watch Ellen DeGeneres stand-up shows. Yes, years before she became like family to me because of Stephen's professional association with her, I was a big fan.

So You Think You Can Dance played a major role in launching dancers into the mainstream, and for that I'll be eternally grateful. No longer were we blurs in the background, eclipsed by musical artists and method actors. With greater visibility came lucrative sponsorships and business opportunities. I was so fortunate to catch the wave of popularity formed by the show and ride it.

SYTYCD is hands down the reason I have four million followers on Instagram. It is hands down the reason that my delusions about making it big as a dancer became a self-fulfilling prophecy. It's because of SYTYCD and Dancing with the Stars that we've been able to reshape the guilds and the SAG-AFTRA rules to give dancers and choreographers more power and agency over their careers.

The show has been the one constant of my adult life, my security blanket. Fans of the show have seen me grow and evolve from a contestant to assistant choreographer to choreographer to dancing with the newbies as a pro to judging. And let's not forget, I also have SYTYCD to thank for bringing me together with the man I would marry.

Stephen was a contestant on Season 4, and then we both appeared as All-Stars in 2010 on Season 7. In my mind, Season 7 is when we met, but that's not technically true. Five years earlier, during my run as a contestant, Ivan hosted a party in Irvine and extended invitations to me, Travis, and another dancer from the show, Natalie Fotopoulos. Ivan had a wide circle of friends, and I was excited to meet them.

One of the people Ivan knew from the hip-hop world approached me during the party. "Hey, I'm tWitch," he said.

tWitch, huh? "That's cute," I said. "What's your real name?"

He appraised me admiringly. He'd been in Los Angeles for a while, he explained, and I was the first person who had asked him that. "Stephen Boss," he replied.

"Okay, well, I'm going to call you Stephen," I said.

Not that it mattered. It was obvious he had a fun energy, but I could not get past his appearance. His fishnet top revealed piercings in both nipples—those in addition to piercings in his nose, eyebrows, lip, and chin. Also, he had dyed his hair blond and was rocking a mohawk! It was too much for this Utah girl, okay?

Stephen was filming the movie *Hairspray* in Toronto at the time, and according to a friend of mine, Sarah Jayne Jensen, who was also in the cast, he was totally geeked out to meet me. He was a *big* admirer of mine, she said. Sarah Jayne and Stephen would join other members of the *Hairspray* cast and crew for weekly *So You Think You Can Dance* viewing parties. Stephen and Sarah Jayne would come dressed as Ivan and me and vote for us every week.

That was sweet, but I wasn't in the market for a boyfriend. I'd been dating someone back home for a year. I was touring and performing in incredible cities like New York and Los Angeles and then reuniting with my nondancer boyfriend in Utah. I had the best of both worlds. I could spread my wings and fly high and far for dance and then return, like a homing pigeon, to my roots. I warmly shook Stephen's hand and went on my merry way. I didn't give our interaction a second thought. I figured we'd probably never run into each other again.

But as they say: I made plans; God laughed.

CHAPTER 4

MY PERFECT ANGEL

Not long after my traumatizing experience, I attended a party hosted by nondance friends. At the end of the night I needed a ride home, as I often did during my teenage years since I didn't have a car or parents available to drive me places. A sweet hunk of a man stepped out of the shadows and volunteered to give me and a few others a lift in his cute red pickup truck. Though Justin (not his real name) was hard to miss at six feet two and two hundred pounds, he had been content to stay in the background all night.

I happened to be the last person Justin dropped off, which I'm pretty sure was by design. I wasn't complaining. He radiated kindness, and by the end of the ride we both sort of implicitly understood that we were dating. He never asked, "Will you be my girlfriend?" He just started driving me everywhere, and we spent as much time together as my schedule would permit.

Justin was older, and he had such a good heart and was so easy to be around. He was quite shy, often struggling to find his voice, but he was sweet, and I instantly felt safe with him. Because of what I'd been through, I was drawn to someone who made me feel protected—and who was not a dancer. I'd sworn off dating other dancers, for multiple reasons.

So I wasn't bothered that Justin didn't like to dance *at all*. I didn't need him to lift me off my feet and twirl me around. What I loved about him was that he grounded me.

Justin was never going to be the life of the party, which was fine because I was vivacious enough for the both of us. Everywhere we went together, he always knew where I was in the room. I always felt like he had his eyes on me in a good way, making sure I was okay. During our drives, I'd draw him out in conversation, which is how we discovered that neither of us had anybody in our day-to-day lives in whom we felt like we could confide. We were both carrying around some heavy baggage, and in each other we found someone willing to help carry the load. We opened up to, and leaned on, each other in a way that neither of us had ever done with anyone else.

Justin's home life, like mine, was not ideal. He hopscotched between his mother's house and his grandmother's place. He had a close relationship with his mom, which I found endearing. He gave her, and me, the best hugs.

One night I stopped by his mother's house to see him. I climbed the stairs to his bedroom, opened the door, and walked in on him seated in a circle with a group of people. The room had a burning chemical odor that I couldn't identify, and everyone's eyes, including Justin's, looked dead, as if all the light had been extinguished from them. I didn't know what I was seeing, but the energy in the room was so scary, I backed out, closed the door, and left.

Later, I asked him what he had been doing with those people, and he admitted he had been using drugs. I broke up with him, but after that we dated off and on. Justin would get clean and sober, I'd be hopeful that we were back on solid ground, and then he'd relapse. Whenever I saw Justin's eyes go dead, that's when I knew he was using again.

What he was doing was really negative, but that didn't make him a bad human being. I never saw the addiction as his; I saw it as something passed down from previous generations, like a defective gene.

During one of our separations, I received word that Justin had gone missing. Nobody had seen or heard from him. I was in LA at the time, so I got on the first flight I could make to Salt Lake City. On a hunch, I drove straight to where I thought he might be staying. I found Justin on the bedroom floor, and it was clear he needed help. His mom and I managed to get him to a detox center. I don't mean a cute, expensive recovery center like the ones in Malibu; I'm talking about a hospital bed with zero privacy where I had to leave him to sweat out the drugs in his system.

Once he had dried out, he decided to go through rehab in Los Angeles, where I was based at the time. I'd go back and forth between work and the recovery center because I wanted to make sure he was being well cared for. I felt obligated to be there for him because I loved him, and I didn't want him to have to bear what he was going through alone. I wanted to carry some of that load for him because, if I'm honest, I wanted him in return to bear some of the load I was carrying.

I wanted to save everyone around me, a pattern that manifested itself in my relationships with both Justin and Stephen. It's in my nature to see the light in people, even if I have to squint. I tend to treat people's struggles not as character flaws but as learning phases that I can help them through. I think it's generally a worthwhile way to live, but sometimes I think I'm just too patient instead of challenging those I love to become healthier versions of themselves.

The armchair therapist in me might hypothesize that because I yearned to be cared for so much, I cared for everyone else. My home life forced me to be so strong and independent, but that didn't mean I didn't wish that Justin—and later, Stephen—would minister to me, take care of me the way I did him.

Justin's drug use made our relationship tumultuous. I couldn't understand the hold the illicit substances had over him. I didn't make the connection that he needed his next hit in kind of the same way that I needed my next performance. Dance, though a much more positive endeavor, was in many ways my coping mechanism—my drug. All I knew was that I loved Justin and I wanted to help him overcome his struggles.

It was really hard to be so close to something so dark. Justin would eventually get and stay sober, but not before I made a silent vow to focus on men who didn't require mothering and were poised to be true partners.

Justin and I had been dating for roughly a year when I auditioned for *So You Think You Can Dance*. He was proud of me but also perplexed by my ambition. We were two very different people. He played it safe in life. He was the rock to my kite, content to stay put while I soared. The sky was the limit for me as a dancer, but Justin was fine with keeping his feet firmly planted on Utah soil. For all the love we shared, we were incompatible in the long run because he was terrified to make a move and I was terrified *not* to make one.

To this day, Justin thinks my life is too complicated. He wonders why I'm always on the go, always on a different set, always pursuing the next job. He has no desire to match my pace, my ambition. Similarly, when I consider his life, I can't imagine staying in one place and working to exist rather than existing to work.

Justin didn't have a career that he was passionate about. Throughout much of our relationship, he struggled to hold a steady job. Toward the end, he would mock my dancing, I think because the breadth of my ambition was intimidating to him. We were a good support system for each other during our time together, but our relationship was never meant to last forever. Like the seasons, it ran its course. But not before bestowing upon us the most beautiful blessing.

After the postseason tour with *SYTYCD*, I was offered a job in New York City. Justin was sober and doing well. I believed in him and trusted that he would stay on the straight and narrow, which he has admirably done to this day. Knowing that he no longer needed me in the same way that he did before, I broke up with him before moving across the country. But after a spell, we reconnected. Justin suggested that we give our relationship another chance. He sent me bouquets of red roses, and we resumed talking every day.

I was proud of him for getting off drugs. And I was so touched by his thoughtfulness that I flew to Utah to visit him during a break from work. I could see the light in his eyes again. I was really grateful that he'd found the strength, after everything he'd been through, to arrive at a place where he had no desire to revisit his addiction. That showed me how brave he is, and I wanted to be there for him. I still cared for him so much. We hooked up once, and just like that, we were a couple again.

Weeks later, I developed a weird craving for orange juice. I don't usually like the stuff, but I downed two gallons. That was strange. After a night spent throwing up, I decided to take a pregnancy test. Surprise! We were going to have a baby.

Justin and I were both thrilled. I had dreamed of being a mother every bit as much as I had dreamed of being a dancer. I wasn't freaked out that I was only nineteen. It had always been my plan to be a young mom. My mother was in her late thirties when I was born, and though we're close now, I don't have many memories of us doing stuff together when I was growing up. I can't recall my mom ever taking me to the park or twirling me around the kitchen. She made it to only a few of my dance performances. She was super supportive but not a hands-on presence in my childhood.

By the time I came along, life had spread her so thin. I wanted to have the connection with my child that I had missed out on with my mom. I wanted to be the most hands-on mother I could be. Nothing else mattered.

Justin's mom was supportive, but I feared how my parents would react to the news. As I saw it, I already had two strikes against me because I had left my religion and led such a flashy and unconventional lifestyle. I suspected that they looked at me and saw a wayward daughter in need of saving.

I was five months along but still hadn't told my parents about my pregnancy when I had a strong urge to visit my paternal grandmother. The best way I can explain it is some magnetic force pulled me to Minnesota, where she lived. I walked into my aunt's house and my grandmother, upon seeing me, pulled me aside straight away. "We need to talk," she said as she dragged me into another room.

My grandmother was known for having supernatural abilities. She was quietly clairvoyant, as she showed when she told a friend it was imperative that she see a doctor immediately and it turned out they were seriously ill. "It's okay," she told me. "Everyone will still love you and your dad will accept you. Your baby girl will be loved."

Understand: I had breathed not a word to her about my pregnancy. And it wasn't as if I was obviously showing. But those were the perfect words at the perfect time. I was so terrified to tell my parents and add another link to the trauma chain that appeared to be the only thing connecting us. My grandmother intuited as much and set about putting my mind at ease.

Shortly after that visit, I flew to Utah and sat them down in the kitchen of the family home. I was so, so, so nervous. But as my grandmother had predicted, both my parents were over the moon to hear about my pregnancy. My dad's face lit up and my mom hugged me hard. They reacted as if it were the most wonderful news ever.

My pregnancy ended up changing the whole trajectory of my relationship with my parents. Our connection became much stronger. It also brought me closer to my siblings, all of whom rallied around me. We had been so preoccupied with our lives that we hadn't been great at keeping in touch. My baby brought everyone back together.

The reaction of my dancing family was decidedly less enthusiastic. One of my bosses at the time, who had always been an unabashed supporter of mine—the first to pitch my name if he was in a room where auditions were taking place—told me my career would be ruined if I had the baby. I revered this man and accepted anything he said as gospel, so I was devastated by his words. And he wasn't alone in his thinking. The consensus seemed to be that the pregnancy, if I was foolish enough to go through with it, would be a career killer. According to my fellow dancers, having a child would signal the end of my professional journey and everything I had worked so hard for.

I'd eventually grow a backbone and stick up for myself when people expressed those kinds of views. I'd always been strong-willed, but there was so much noise in the dance world surrounding my situation that I couldn't drown out all the voices. I started to believe them.

I danced until my last trimester, which is when I really started to show, and then I returned to Utah. It was easy to rationalize the move because it made sense to be with Justin for the baby's birth. My decision gave ammunition to both the naysayers in New York, who saw my departure as permanent, and my parents in Utah, who'd never stopped believing that I'd return home for good one day.

Around this time, I had cause to question if my grandmother's clairvoyance was something we had in common. Justin and I were undecided on a name for our daughter, though we had narrowed our choices, when I had a dream one night in which our baby appeared to me as a ten-year-old and announced, "I'm Weslie." I woke up with a start, sat up straight in bed, and shouted, "Her name is Weslie! Our daughter is Weslie." I can still vividly see her face from that dream.

I was twenty when Weslie, my perfect angel, was born on May 26, 2008, weighing eight pounds, five ounces. As I settled into motherhood, I did my best to banish all thoughts about the career I had left behind. For the first time, I found myself believing the limitations others were projecting onto me. I questioned my instincts and made space for the possibility that I might never dance professionally again. I felt like I stood not at a crossroads but at a dead end. I entertained the idea of going to college and getting a "real" job, though I had no idea what that would look like.

After Weslie was born, Justin and I rented a quaint, old craftsman cottage in Pleasant Grove, Utah. The house was tiny, but it sat on a half-acre lot. It gave off Pioneer Woman vibes, which was a 180-degree change from the life I left behind in New York. We were fortunate to be able to tap into a government program, WIC, the Special Supplemental Nutrition Program for Women, Infants, and Children. Although this wasn't the start I had envisioned for Weslie, it was our reality. My desire that she would never know the financial insecurity that I grew up with motivated me to complete college applications.

I knew I wanted to be a good mom, so I felt no resentment whatsoever toward Weslie. I told myself I was exactly where I should be. But as I nourished her, I began starving the parts of myself that made me the person I was in the world. I wasn't even old enough to legally drink and I was having an existential crisis. Who was I? My confidence was badly shaken. I started to lose myself. *Maybe it's silly for me to want to be a dancer*, I thought. I asked myself, *Who do I think I am to believe I can juggle being a choreographer and a mother?* I stopped telling Justin about my dreams of resuming my career because I couldn't imagine how I'd pull it off.

The love and intense bond I felt with Weslie from her first breath is indescribable. I'm convinced we somehow must have shared a past life. Our journey hasn't been easy, but it has always felt as if Weslie was destined to be by my side for it. She emerged from my womb with a fun, bubbly personality, and as soon as she entered our lives, I realized it was true what they say about motherhood: It is like having your heart beating outside your body.

Weslie had my heart from the start. There was nothing I wouldn't do for her. I settled into a quieter, smaller life than the big, lavish world I had inhabited as a dancer.

I had a fur baby at the time, a Pomeranian named Harley who was my pride and joy until Weslie came along. I was one of those annoying people who carried my dog around in my purse wherever I went. Justin proposed to me by attaching the engagement ring to Harley's collar and then standing back with a huge grin on his face while Harley ran to me. But even as I accepted his offer of marriage, I knew in my gut that we'd never make it to the altar.

I felt safe with Justin, but his contentment with the status quo was a sticking point for me. I came to realize during all my laps around our block slow-walking Weslie in her stroller that I had lost myself. I wasn't dancing all over the world. I wasn't working out. I wasn't hanging out with friends. I had dropped out of the dance world. I had left my religion. I wasn't really part of any community. My world had become suffocatingly small.

On my walks with Weslie, I would chastise myself for not living up to the promise that my mom and Sheryl had seen and supported. I was present for Weslie, but I otherwise felt like I was just going through the motions. I'd had a glimpse of the wider world, and I didn't want to be constrained to a half-acre plot in Utah for the rest of my life. I had passively accepted my new place in life, dimming my light and holding myself back because I didn't want to disrupt the peace by challenging accepted norms. But I couldn't turn off half of myself to keep my little family of three together.

I wanted more for us. Not just materially; I wanted a bigger life. I wanted to succeed to be a model of strength and perseverance for our daughter. Whereas I had once seen dance as my purpose, after Weslie was born my purpose expanded. I realized it was my responsibility to be an example to her that she can survive adversity and become anything she dreams of being in the world. I couldn't give up on myself because I had to teach her by word and deed how to not just survive but thrive.

Our savings had run out, so I began sending feelers out for dancing jobs. Pretty soon I was back working conventions on the weekends. I'm not going to lie: It was brutal being a young working mother. When I was on the road, other dancers would ask me, "Where's your daughter?" I wanted to be snarky and say something like, "Oh, shoot, I left her at the airport!" Justin wasn't going to a job every day and yet nobody, at least not that I know of, asked him why he was dropping Weslie off at my mom's every morning even when he wasn't working.

I'd explain that my daughter was with my mother, but that didn't keep people from judging my decision. I'd hear variations of, "Don't you think you should choose another path?" When I was pressed about why I was working when I had a child back at home, I said that I needed the work. I'd explain that I was her sole source of financial support. These conversations would lay me low sometimes. I would tell myself, *There are doctors who are mothers. There are writers who are mothers. Why can't I be a dancer who's a mother?*

Around this time, I received a life-changing piece of advice from a crew member at one of the handful of dance conventions I was working. He noticed one weekend that I was subdued and seemed sad. He gave me an affirmation—*I am . . . I have . . . I deserve . . .* —and advised me to finish the sentences and say them out loud while staring into a mirror. I was to repeat them over and over until I believed the words.

I had been doing affirmations for a while, but literally facing myself while doing so was a new rub.

I didn't stop there. Soon I was filling entire pages in my journals with sentences that started with "I am . . .": *I am strong. I am smart. I am beautiful. I am kind. I am patient. I am loving. I am a good mom. I am a powerful influence in the world of dance.* You get the picture. Two years later, after I began dating Stephen, he saw me scribbling in my journal and asked what I was writing. After I told him about the affirmation, he had *I am . . . I have . . . I deserve . . .* tattooed on his left bicep.

My biggest dream was to own a house. As the paychecks rolled in, I did the math and came up with what I thought was a bright idea. If I hustled for two or three months, traveling nonstop for work (on the road, all my expenses were paid), I could make enough money for a down payment on a property. As a child whose parents were evicted from homes for not being able to pay the rent, I wanted my daughter to have a greater sense of security.

Justin worked on and off, and when he landed a job in construction or welding—he was good at both—my mom pitched in to watch Weslie. I had been on the road for less than a month when I fielded a call from Justin's boss. He asked, "How's Justin?"

How did I know? I wasn't home. "Oh, he's doing okay," I said, treading cautiously. "What's going on?"

"Well, he's not at work."

That was certainly news to me. Striving to keep my voice neutral, I said, "Oh, I know. He wasn't feeling well today. I'm so sorry he didn't call."

"Here's the thing," his boss added. "He hasn't shown up for work at all."

I didn't know what to say. I thanked him and said I'd talk to Justin. I immediately called my mother and asked her if Justin had dropped Weslie off at her house that morning. She said he had, and that he had been dressed in his work clothes and boots.

I resolved to find out what was going on. I booked the next flight back to Salt Lake City and flew home. Because we were trying to save money, we had given up the quaint cottage and were living in the basement of the home where Justin's mom lived. I went to his mom's house, descended the stairs, and there Justin was, playing video games and surrounded by so many empty wrappers it looked as if he had cleaned out the snack aisle of a gas station convenience store.

"What's going on?" I asked.

"I didn't go to work today, but everything's good," he said.

"Don't lie to me," I said. "Your boss called. I already know you never started the job." I was beside myself. I cut to the chase: "Would you want someone like you for Weslie?"

"No," Justin said. No, he would not.

I left. On my way out I had one more surprise awaiting me. While I was out on the road making money so we could buy a house, Justin had gone out and bought a small lightweight motorcycle that he had parked outside.

Justin had a kind heart, and he really did aspire to be a good dad. He has remained sober to this day, which is a herculean feat that reveals so much about his character. But when you have a kid, you have to grow up. I thought he would, but he just wasn't ready.

I broke off our engagement, which was heartbreaking. I never wanted to hurt Justin, and I'll always love him. He gave me our beautiful daughter, who has greatly enhanced both our lives. And I'm enormously proud of his continued sobriety. We just had different life goals. I felt like I had become his mother, setting his work clothes out for him, making his lunches, and checking up on him to see that he made it to his job. At the end of the day, I knew it was selfish of me to be with him because I wasn't fully invested in our relationship. That didn't keep me from sobbing. Nor did it prevent Justin from crying and begging me not to go.

I moved forward with my plan to attend college, but I kept hitting metaphorical red lights. In retrospect, it was the universe's way of saying I was heading in the wrong direction. I finally completed my application to Utah Valley University in Orem, where my plan was to study child psychology. The envelope was sealed, stamped, and ready to be dropped off at the post office when I received an unexpected call from Jeff Thacker, the producer of *So You Think You Can Dance*. He offered me a job on the show as an All-Star, a group composed of a dozen of the most popular dancers from seasons past.

Though I was incredibly flattered to be one of the chosen, I turned down the offer. I was out of shape, on government assistance, and only months removed from a broken engagement. In my mind, I in no way resembled the sparkling teenager from Season 2.

It gutted me to pass on the opportunity. But even if I thought I could regain my dancing form, what was I going to do with Weslie? Leaving her with Justin wasn't an option, and he was never going to leave the security of Utah to move with me to LA.

That night, I poured my heart out to my mom. I expected her to support my decision. To my astonishment, she told me life was presenting me with a gift: a chance to reclaim a vital aspect of my identity. Before I could love Weslie, she added, I needed to first love and honor myself, and the only way I could do that was by remaining true to my calling, which was dance.

I wouldn't have been the first woman to relinquish her primary identity after becoming a mother because she thought she had to squeeze herself into a stifling box for the sake of her children. But I imagined a future conversation I might have with Weslie in which I'd encourage her to dream big and live expansively. Did I want her to grow up seeing me as a hypocrite, or as someone who walked my talk?

My conversation with my mom reignited a flame that I thought had been extinguished. I decided I could, and would, be the best dancing parent on the planet. I promptly called Jeff back and rescinded my no. I said I'd be honored to be an All-Star. It was a decision, and conversation, that would result in my life becoming bigger than I could have ever imagined.

CHAPTER 5

STEPHEN

I f *Step Up* had been a documentary instead of a musical romance, Stephen and I would have been shoo-ins for the lead roles. Like Chase and Andie in the 2008 film, we came from different backgrounds and weathered all manner of drama to be together. The plot of our movie would have looked something like this: Boy meets girl. Girl rebuffs boy. Girl reassesses boy but a series of comical misconnections keeps them from getting together. Boy and girl finally dance with each other—and it's magic.

Not for nothing, it was at the *Step Up 3D* premiere that Stephen, who was in the film, *finally* asked for my number. And then didn't call me.

But I'm getting ahead of myself.

My move to LA was a high-stakes play in every conceivable way. The *So You Think You Can Dance* job guaranteed me income for only three months, so I had to hustle for more work or risk returning to Utah with my tail between my legs. Before I left home, my mother, recognizing the gravity of the situation, encouraged me to write down my top ten career goals to help me sustain my focus amid the bright lights of the big city. Her suggestion worked so well that I would end up hosting annual goal-writing parties for my friends. At the end of my first year, I had already checked off six or seven of the items on my list, everything short of appearing on Broadway and dancing in a world tour.

I was used to traveling with all the advance planning of a hitchhiker. I operated by the seat of my pants. If I was working an out-of-town gig, I thought nothing of crashing on a friend's couch. But moving to another state with a baby was next-level adulting. I had to put away money so that Weslie could maintain a commuter relationship with her dad through twice-monthly visits to Utah. I had to find a quiet and affordable apartment close to the studio where the show was being shot, somewhere also near a grocery store and park. And I had to find someone cheap yet reliable to look after Weslie when I was working. I lucked out when I secured an apartment with a landlord who, bless his heart, treated me like his daughter. He came to my aid whenever I had a concern or question or clogged pipes. And through an internet site, I hired a nanny who was only a year older than me and also a recent arrival to LA. She was able to accommodate my chaotic dance schedule and the cut-rate salary I offered, which was all I could afford.

Having emptied my down-payment savings to secure the apartment, I was forever pinching pennies. I did my best to stretch my paycheck. I was an amateur magician pulling an endless amount of dollar bills from my wallet like so many colored silk scarves out of a top hat. My goal every week was to put aside ten dollars a day and use that money to treat Weslie to a trip to a museum or the zoo or a mother-daughter manicure.

I'd also seek out creative—which is to say, free—forms of entertainment, like browsing at The Grove, an outdoor mall, or the La Brea farmers market. I knew when every free children's story time took place at all the nearby libraries and bookstores. We became regulars at La Brea Tar Pits and Museum and the Los Angeles County Museum of Art. We never bought anything, but we could make a nice day of it by packing sandwiches from home and bringing bottled water. We didn't have much money, but we never felt poor because Weslie and I had the greatest gift of all: each other.

As I auditioned for jobs as a dancer or choreographer, I became painfully aware of how few mothers and fathers were working in the industry. It was little wonder why. Everywhere I went, I was subjected to snide remarks and invasive comments, such as, "Are you breastfeeding?" I learned to take in stride backhanded compliments like, "You're an exceptional dancer *and* mother. I never expected that!"

At auditions, I'd be asked, "You have a kid, so how does that work? Will you have to leave early?" I'd patiently explain that I was like any other working mom who arranges childcare and manages her responsibilities. Of course, if a true emergency arose, I'd need to leave. It frustrated me that so many prospective bosses looked at me and saw a migraine waiting to happen.

I was passed over for a few jobs that I couldn't afford to lose because of an assumption, then common in the industry, that someone without the responsibility of a child would be more committed to their work. I learned to downplay the fact that I had a daughter, never volunteering the information, which made me ashamed. I was hiding a significant part of who I was to sidestep the profession's ingrained sexism and backward thinking.

The eleven other All-Stars on *So You Think You Can Dance* included the now mohawk-less Stephen. He sported a much cleaner look than when we had met at Ivan's party, and without his hair or piercings distracting me, I couldn't help but notice that he was awfully cute. I was shocked when Stephen's eyes seemed to linger on me during rehearsals. He'd flash me sly smiles from across the room. Could it be that this high-quality human was *flirting* with me?

Given my complex situation, I didn't consider myself prime dating material. Far from it! Why would any man in his right mind choose to wade into my business?

Since meeting Stephen at Ivan's party, I had followed his work. He was so talented. I loved to watch him dance. I even brought Weslie to one of Stephen's performances, but I had to get her home to bed so I didn't have the opportunity to talk to him and the other dancers after the show. Comparing notes later, we realized we'd had numerous near misses. We'd be at the same parties but not at the same time, or we'd dance after each other in shows. It was almost as if the universe kept us from meeting until we were both in the right headspace and the right place in our lives to be open to receiving each other.

Stephen won me over—bowled me over, really—during a *SYTYCD* rehearsal in which he was paired with a first-time contestant. As I sat on the sidelines watching them practice, what struck me was his approach. Instead of patronizing her or offering excessive critiques, he showered her with encouragement and constructive feedback. His interactions with her came from a place of kindness and respect, as if she were a precious gem. Stephen's behavior was that of a true gentleman. He was supportive, warm, and considerate. He carried himself with integrity. Witnessing him nurture and guide another person like that made him super attractive in my eyes. Right then and there, I felt an instant connection, a certainty that he was the kindest human being I'd ever come across.

My infatuation with Stephen caused me to reconsider my vow not to date dancers. I concluded that I'd make an exception in his case. I was crushing on him so hard. His personality was so fun, and he oozed authenticity. Throughout our journey—from fame and success to marriage and parenthood—that purity of spirit never left him.

Throughout the season, I made clear my interest in Stephen in myriad ways. I'd brush up against him any chance I got and coo, "Hey." At rehearsal, I'd find ways to make gentle physical contact. I'd murmur, "You missed a few eight counts. Let me show you." But Stephen seemed completely oblivious. Little did I know how closely he was paying attention. For instance, it did not escape his notice that I was hosting parties on the weekends that cast members would rave about after the fact— parties that he had no prior knowledge of. For all my extroversion, I was too shy to invite him because I liked him so much. I didn't think I could ask him without blushing, and what if he said no? Rather than risk being crushed, I chose cowardice.

Much later, when we were officially a couple, he blamed his seeming indifference on low self-esteem. He said he was afraid that if he said hello or made a move that demonstrated his interest and I didn't respond, his shame and embarrassment would have been acute. Which made us more alike than either of us realized. Plus, by his own admission, he wasn't great at reading women. Like me, he never considered himself a prize catch.

The All-Stars attended the *Step Up 3D* Hollywood premiere in August 2010. Stephen, because he was in the movie's cast, arrived separately from the rest of us. I saw him standing on the red carpet in a nice gray suit, and my heart skipped a beat. At the after-party, I met his mom and brother and danced with Stephen. Not only did he try to impress me by showing off his moves on the dance floor, but he also slipped off his shirt while staring at me like he was Patrick Swayze in *Dirty Dancing*. It was a very un-Stephen-like gesture, and I loved it. To my delight, he asked for my phone number.

The idea that someone like Stephen, who undoubtedly had the ability to choose from a multitude of women, would be interested in a single mom was mind-boggling to me. But then I didn't hear from him. He'd tell people later that he dismissed my friendliness toward him as a natural consequence of my being a "social butterfly extraordinaire," as he put it. Whatever. The bottom line is he never reached out, and I stopped expecting to hear from him. I did my best to move on.

We officially got together at the Season 7 wrap party for *SYTYCD*. The funny thing is, I hadn't planned to attend. The event was held at a club off Melrose Avenue, and I have never been a nightclub kind of girl. My mom was visiting, so I decided to stay home and hang out with her and Weslie. We were contemplating what type of pizza to order for delivery when Stephen texted me, *finally*, to see if I was going to be at the party. My mom encouraged me to go. Within minutes, I was flinging clothes around my closet in search of the perfect outfit.

Walking into the club, I felt like I had stepped into a scene straight out of a movie. As I let the vibe wash over me, I glanced over at the stairs and there was Stephen, standing at the top. He pointed at me and beckoned me with his outstretched arms to join him. I did. Without saying a word, he grabbed my hand and led me down to the dance floor. Usher's "Yeah!" started playing, and from the first beat we were grooving on the dance floor. Our styles collided, and it got wild.

We were all over each other. Our attraction was magnetic. It was like we were in our own snow globe. Everyone else at the party fell away. It's hilarious to look at photographs from that night because everyone was staring at us in disbelief. I was pretty surprised myself. We shared our first kiss on the dance floor. Oh, who am I kidding? We were fully making out.

Eventually, Stephen took my hand and led me away from the crowd. He pinned me against the elevator. We were so lost in our own world, skin on skin, that we had no idea that we were blocking people from getting into the elevator.

After midnight, as the party was petering out, Stephen and I were dancing on tables. I took a minute to text my mom to say, "I think I'm going home with this guy." Her reply was succinct: "DO IT." Which is so not like my mom! She knew that I liked Stephen, and she trusted that he was a good guy.

Stephen had a classic bachelor pad in North Hollywood that screamed tWitch. There was a bright red wall with a ginormous Superman logo. I kid you not. That morning, he drove me home in his black, box-shaped Scion while holding my hand.

And that was that. We were together from then on. As had been the case with Justin, Stephen never asked me to be his girlfriend. I just *was*.

It quickly became clear to me that Stephen was two distinct people: the gregarious, joyful performer with a generous spirit and a "50,000-watt smile" per our friend, television personality Carson Daly (he wasn't wrong)—and the inherently quiet and reserved loner who experienced social anxiety.

The performer was tWitch. And if you ever saw him swivel around in his rolling chair and gesticulate like a symphony conductor when he talked, you instantly understood why the nickname followed him into adulthood. I was in awe of tWitch. When he moved, the floor beneath him shook. He was a hard, aggressive dancer, but his strength was his sensitivity. He exuded such love, it was as if he said through his movements, *Hey, everyone, I'm home. Come on in. I'll leave the light on.*

But it was Stephen with whom I fell deeply in love. Even beyond our physical attraction, Stephen and I connected on an almost cellular level. On the surface, we didn't seem to have much in common, the Black hip-hop dancer from the Deep South and the white contemporary dancer from Utah. And yet, as soon as we began talking, we quickly realized how much our childhoods were alike. We both grew up feeling like the oddball or outcast in our communities. We talked extensively about the loneliness of not fitting in, of feeling out of your element in the place you call home, the place where you presumably should feel the most secure. It was lovely to connect with someone on such a deep level. It was like, *Wow. You feel this way too?*

I didn't fit in because I was a poor kid surrounded by so much affluence in the world of dance, and then because of the religion I renounced and the traumatizing incident that further isolated me. Stephen, who grew up in Montgomery, Alabama, also had trauma and abandonment issues from his childhood. He carried invisible scars that he hinted about to me but never directly addressed. His mother and father had never married, and I know he grew up feeling as if his father resented his presence. His feelings of being forsaken or forgotten intensified after his father married another woman, who bore him a son whom he doted on. Stephen internalized his biological dad's disinterest in him as evidence that he must be fundamentally unlovable. How else to explain his father lavishing all his time and attention on his second son? He got the attention he craved by becoming the class clown, which fueled his interest in theater and eventually dance.

In high school, when Stephen asked his father, who had played football, for money for dance shoes, he was rebuffed. Football cleats? No problem. But dance shoes? What kind of a sissy did he have who aspired to be the only boy on the high school dance team? His dad, Stephen acknowledged several years later in an interview with the football player–turned-podcaster Lewis Howes, wasn't actively involved in his life. If he had been, who knows, Stephen said ruefully. "I might have been clashing helmets with you."

Like me, Stephen had been engaged to be married for the first time when he was nineteen. As a junior studying dance performance at Southern Union State Community College in Wadley, Alabama, he fell madly in love with a white girl who was not allowed to date Black men. Stephen proposed, but the relationship fell apart because his fiancée wasn't willing to disclose the relationship to her family. Following the breakup, Stephen decided to follow his dreams to Los Angeles, just as I had. He described himself as "untrained" when, in fact, he attended Chapman University, an Orange County school with an excellent dance program, on scholarship and started auditioning for anything and everything.

My conversations with Stephen got deep fast. We talked about the different cultures that formed us and the challenges we'd face navigating both as a couple. He talked about why he knew he could be with somebody like me, and I talked about why I knew I could be with somebody like him. A couple of weeks into dating, we were already discussing our mutual love language: physical touch, with its emphasis on hugging, holding hands, and cuddling. We both needed to give, and receive, love that way. We also both thrived on words of affirmation. From the beginning, we talked extensively and honestly about race and religion and manifestations and self-help and future goals—where we were and where we wanted to be.

Both of us wanted big lives. We had audacious bucket lists. High on mine was skydiving. When I mentioned that to Stephen, he tucked the information away. On the morning of my next birthday—this was before we were married—he steered me to the car and told me that he had a big surprise for me. "Where are we going?" I asked. He said he couldn't tell me. It was a surprise. Two hours later, we pulled up to a skydiving drop zone. I was ecstatic. I remember thinking, *This is actually happening!*

There were maybe ten of us jumping, and once we were settled in our places in the plane, I looked over at Stephen, who was totally panicking. He was trying so hard to be supportive of me, but he was extremely nervous. As soon as we reached the jumping altitude and the door swung open, one of the instructors shouted, "Who wants to go first?" I did, naturally. I leaned over and kissed Stephen—then *Poof!* I was gone. Stephen later told me his heart dropped when he saw me disappear into the big blue yonder. It was kind of scary at first, but as soon as the parachute opened, the trip down was spectacular, offering me a thrilling perspective of nature and of Earth. It was such an invigorating experience that, as soon as I touched the ground, my first thought was, *I want to do that again!*

I waited for Stephen to land and then we collapsed on the grass, both of us emotionally drained, and lay there for several minutes talking about what we had just experienced. From the start, we were up for any adventure.

Early in our relationship, our romance was conducted mostly through AOL Instant Messenger and email. Stephen was touring as part of a dance ensemble opening act for *Glee*, and I was on the *So You Think You Can Dance* tour following Season 7. There was one memorable meetup at the O₂ indoor amphitheater in Dublin, where the *Glee* cast was performing. Stephen was done for the night after performing with the Legion of Extraordinary Dancers under the direction of Jon Chu (remember that name), so we spent the rest of the concert exploring the arena. We ended up in the scaffolding above the stage—don't ask me how—and started making out. One thing led to another until we were in flagrante delicto. I can't lie. It was one of the hottest things I've ever done. We were almost caught in the act by a security guard who appeared out of nowhere, shined his flashlight near us, and announced, "Who's up here?" We stifled giggles until the coast was clear, then hastily got dressed and rejoined the concertgoers.

We danced our faces off at concerts from coast to coast. We loved going to hear live music together. Another of our favorite things to do was mute the volume on a foreign language movie or show and make up our own dialogue. We could be such children. We also loved sending each other riddles. I can still remember this one: Every morning a man wakes up and turns his lights off. Every night before he goes to bed, he turns his lights on. Why is this? Answer: Because he is a lighthouse keeper.

In every respect, Stephen and I were totally on the same page. And if that page had black ink on white paper, so what? I'm not suggesting that I was colorblind. Of course I was aware of Stephen's melanin pigments and the way his skin color impacted how he experienced the world. I'd never speak from a place of not noticing color. I saw him as a beautiful Black man. It just didn't matter to me that we were different races. But it quickly became evident after we started dating that it was a problem, one thousand percent, in the Black and white communities that spawned us.

People made awful comments on social media. Black people, white people—we heard it from both sides: I was insensitive to the Black culture; I had no business dating outside my race; I was going straight to hell and dragging Stephen along with me. Our supporters outnumbered our critics, but man oh man, the mean-spiritedness lurked under every social media post and around every corner.

Any time we traveled to Montgomery to visit Stephen's family or went to certain other places in the South, we knew to avoid certain restaurants. At Stephen's suggestion, we'd order room service rather than dine out. Even in a city as cosmopolitan as New York, there'd be times he'd have to hold me real close because he intuited a threat I couldn't see.

There were moments of ugliness I was too naive to anticipate. Although I had friends of every race and religion, I'd never personally experienced racism until I was with Stephen. As we were going through security at the airport for the first flight we took together, a white passenger accused Stephen of wanting to steal his belongings. I was horrified. I couldn't believe my eyes or ears. Stephen calmly walked away from the situation. I didn't understand why he didn't give the man a piece of his mind. Stephen explained that he couldn't react because to do so would be to come across as the person the man was projecting him to be.

I was crushed that anyone would ever treat someone, let alone Stephen, so rudely. It had never crossed my mind that there might be people who'd want to hurt, or hate, us simply because we were a couple. We could forgive them their intolerance—we were never going to let them defeat us—but we would never forget. In June 2020, Stephen and I took to our respective Instagram pages to celebrate the fifty-third anniversary of the *Loving v. Virginia* Supreme Court case. Two Virginia residents, Mildred Jeter and Richard Loving, had married in the District of Columbia. After returning to Virginia, they were charged with violating the state's anti-miscegenation statute and sentenced to one year in jail. In a unanimous decision, the Court struck down the laws that banned interracial marriage.

Stephen posted a photo of Jeter, a Black woman, and Loving, her white husband, alongside a photo of us on our wedding day. "Love wins. 53 years ago today, our life together became a possibility," he wrote. "Forever turned into reality. Our family, our legacy. We couldn't have gotten here without Mr. & Mrs. Loving." He added, "And just like their love for each other paved the way for change, I want for our love to do the same. To be a picture of hope. A picture of happiness. A picture that ACTUALLY looks like a really dope puzzle. Like, pieces that at one time were apart indefinitely, until someone said, 'nah, there's a bigger picture here.' Building that picture takes patience. Humility. Focus. Optimism. Vision. Steadfastness."

There wasn't a whole lot I could add to that beautiful tribute. "I was able to marry the love of my life," I wrote, "because Mr & Mrs LOVING showed us that love always wins! 53 years ago they became the first interracial marriage to become legal! I am grateful and will continue to move forward with love!" Pretty innocuous, right? Not to the commenters who came to our pages and timelines to torch us, saying that we shouldn't be allowed to marry or have children.

Honestly, sometimes the opposition came from the unlikeliest places—like a women's bathroom in North Hollywood. Stephen and I hadn't been going out long when we showed up at a restaurant called the

Federal that was located in an old bank building. On the second level, there was a dance floor that attracted the heavy hitters in the industry. It was our equivalent of a basketball court where cutthroat pickup games broke out. There were regularly events where you'd see professional dancers going toe to toe.

Our relationship was very new, very fresh. Word was just getting out that we were a couple. I left the dance floor to go to the bathroom and ran into two women. I'm not going to say their names, bless their little hearts, but they're huge in the dance industry. They both got in my face and started hurling insults at me. I remember their diatribe unfurling something like this: "Whatcha think you're doing here? You're taking one of our own. You're taking one of the good ones. You're a white girl; you don't know how to handle this man. How dare you? You don't represent us. You can't understand what it's like. How dare you do this to our culture? He's never going to get you. You're never going to get him."

One of them said that Stephen should be with her instead. I waited until they were out of breath. And then I said, "Look, I'm just trying to go pee."

Returning to the dance floor after doing my business, I was weaving my way through a sea of people toward Stephen when suddenly a hand clamped down on my shoulder. I turned to see who the hand belonged to and came face-to-face with one of my toilet-room tormentors. She started krumping, and a circle formed around us because she was going crazy, pushing people away to make room for her aggressive, almost combative, dancing. I'd never really danced hip-hop, and I'd certainly never tried krumping—I'd never even seen it done before. I turned to Stephen, who by this time had made his way to my side, and I was so excited. I said, "She's battling me. What do I do?" See, I saw it not as a mean-girl challenge but as a mano a mano competition. I was flattered beyond belief. I considered it the coolest thing ever that someone wanted to battle me on the dance floor, like in the movies. I was down for it!

True to his nature, Stephen replied, "Don't worry, baby. I've got this."

He pulled me back, stepped into the circle, and started battling her. They went back and forth, taking turns frenetically swinging their arms and shimmying their shoulders and shuffling their feet as the crowd that had gathered around them went wild. Stephen destroyed her, then flung his arm across my shoulder and escorted me off the floor and out of the building.

CHAPTER 6

ONE AND ONLY

Whereas Stephen and I dived headfirst into our relationship, I was hesitant for a long time to facilitate his bonding with Weslie. As a single mom navigating the dating world, I was protecting us both. I was uncertain what the future held, and Weslie was my number one priority. I didn't want her to grow attached to someone who might not stick around.

In the spring of 2011, when Weslie was two and Stephen and I had been dating for a few months, Stephen expressed a desire to forge a relationship with her that went beyond reading the occasional bedtime story. I agreed the timing felt right. As it happened, I was working on two shows—VH1's *Hit the Floor* and a reality TV series called *All the Right Moves* that aired on the Oxygen network—and my mom was helping a lot with childcare because my days were endless.

Stephen stepped in and one day offered to escort Weslie on a playdate. He took her to the Grove and they walked around, eventually ending up at the movie *Hop*, where they shared popcorn and laughs. From that day forward, they had a special connection.

Stephen was really good about staying in his lane. He had no designs on replacing Justin in Weslie's life. He respected the sanctity of Weslie's bond with her biological father, and I think that's a big reason why he and Justin got along so well. Every time they'd see each other, they'd do that bro salute, the half-handshake, half-high-five, one-armed-hug-slash-shoulder-bump greeting.

We knew we wanted to take it slow, be patient, and let Weslie's relationship with Stephen evolve organically. Evidence that we were on the right track came when Weslie was around five. During a conversation in the car, she casually referred to Stephen as "Dad." Stephen and I exchanged glances. We were delighted, but we didn't want to make a big deal of it. We always wanted Weslie to have a sense of agency over her environment, probably because neither of us had it growing up.

We divided daily responsibilities like taking Weslie to elementary school and preparing her lunches. Stephen embraced every moment and was eager to make sure he was doing everything right as a father. He became her second daddy, and she became his "ace." He actually called her that: "my ace." Why? I have no idea. I never wanted to risk making him feel self-conscious by asking.

Stephen's paternal instincts were sound, yet he often struggled with the feeling that he wasn't doing enough. He seemed so determined to break his family's generational cycle of abuse and neglect that I think he expected too much of himself. He wanted to be a "perfect parent"—whatever that looks like. He doubted his competence even when I reassured him that he was a natural at fatherhood.

In 2012, Weslie and I moved in with Stephen, who was renting a two-bedroom townhouse in North Hollywood. The first of three floors, accessible from the one-car garage, basically was taken up by the washer and dryer and all of Stephen's Superman memorabilia, though there was enough room for Weslie to choreograph a dance to a Justin Bieber song.

As is the case with most couples, living under the same roof brought into sharp focus the differences in our personalities. I love to entertain. I'm invigorated by social interactions. Stephen was the complete opposite. Away from the spotlight, he was painfully shy. He would become terribly nervous ahead of red-carpet events and the like. Once back home, he'd say, "I need a second." He'd cinch the hoodie strings so that his head and ears were completely covered and retreat into himself in the dark—like a turtle into its shell—while seated in his favorite chair.

It never dawned on me that Stephen's shyness could be a manifestation of social anxiety disorder. I'm not sure it would have made a difference if I had realized it. Whenever I asked him if there was anything I could do to be of assistance, he'd say, "I don't need help. I just need a moment to recharge myself."

His comfort with clutter, which clashed with my desire for neatness and order, I saw as endearing, not exasperating. I joked about how I could always tell where Stephen had been in the house because he would leave a trail of clothes and dishes and journals and books and beanies in his wake. I was forever picking up after him. "Allison is so clean," Stephen would say. "She's so organized." The way he said it, I wasn't sure he meant it as a compliment. Clutter, I've since learned, can be a trauma response. Stephen could have been either distracting himself with all his stuff or erecting a physical barricade to block out painful memories.

After I moved in, Stephen impulsively bought a hideous sectional even though he had to have known that we had no space for it anywhere. He'd do that a lot—buy stuff on a whim. The sectional ended up in our bedroom because it was the only place it fit—and then just barely. It took up so much space it was impossible to close the door. Stephen considered it the greatest setup ever because he could literally roll from his bed to the sectional first thing in the morning and play video games with minimal effort.

As I slowly upgraded the bachelor décor with my own personal design, executed on the cheap, Stephen complimented my style. He called me the "gangsta of design" but said he'd prefer our house messier.

Stuff gave him a sense of security. He was a big collector, accumulating hoodies, hats, sneakers, action figures, and Lego bricks. He'd create dioramas with Legos and plastic figurines and display them on the counter or on a high shelf. He'd attach an action figure to a pendant light. Nobody was allowed to mess with his toys. I kid you not, he created his Instagram account not so he could show off his dance moves but to display his Lego creations. His first post was of his toys. That childlike quality was adorable, I thought. I accepted all his weird behaviors because they were what made Stephen Stephen.

My attitude was *You do you*. And Stephen was a big kid. In the morning, he'd consume two or three bowls of cereal, either Cinnamon Toast Crunch or Frosted Mini-Wheats. Not the diet that most dancers would endorse, but it worked for Stephen, so who was I to question him? He loved spicy food, especially an Asian brand of ramen noodles, even though to look at him while he was consuming it, it didn't seem to agree with him. We would sit around the table and giggle as he sweated profusely while professing his love of food with a kick to it.

He ascribed to his "sensitive taste palate" his weird habit of eating a meal one food group at a time—for example, all the meat, then the starch, followed by the vegetables. Whatever it was, it was not a sophisticated palate. Wherever we traveled, I'd be eager to sample the local cuisine while Stephen was content to hole up in our hotel room and order every meal from room service.

Then there was his habit of leaving the cap off the toothpaste. Every single morning in our early days together I'd shuffle into the bathroom and there'd be a glob of toothpaste spilling out of the tube and onto the counter. And every single day I'd call him out on it. "Why can't you do this simple thing for me?" I would say. Eventually, he started putting the cap on, which triggered one of *my* eccentricities: I discovered that cleaning up his toothpaste mess was another of my love languages. I missed doing it, and after a few days I practically begged him to go back to leaving the tube uncapped.

In retrospect, Stephen's quirks hit a little differently. I was only twenty-two years old when we started dating, and there are so many things that you overlook when you're that age because you are young and dumb and blinded by love. It was easy for me to look at his quirkiness as part of his charm. He came across as a perfectly functional adult, but inside he was a forlorn seven-year-old. I feel terrible that I couldn't see how hard he must have been trying on his own to heal his wounded inner child. As tWitch, he could access the confidence, innocence, and joy that is every child's birthright. But Stephen couldn't address the sadness and anger he had learned at a young age to repress. He wouldn't even acknowledge their existence.

Stephen spread compliments like bees do pollen. But he was terrible at accepting praise, returning it to the sender as quickly as he could. Perhaps Stephen was quick to shift the attention onto other people because the more he focused on everyone else, the less he fixated on himself. He was the first to acknowledge how easy it was for him to slip into his head and stay there.

Every morning Stephen would bring me coffee in bed. How lucky was I? I thought it was so sweet of him. All my friends agreed. But there was more going on than met the eye. It took me a long time to figure out that that beautiful gesture was his signal that I had his permission to come downstairs and start my day. The pieces fell into place when we were the harried parents of three living in a sprawling house in Encino. One day, inspired by a podcast on productivity I had listened to, I suggested to him that I should rise when he did, at six, and get my workout done before the children woke up. That wouldn't work, Stephen said, explaining that he'd then have to get up at five. He needed that undisturbed hour alone downstairs. It was nonnegotiable.

If I stayed upstairs during that hour but got out of bed, he would chide me for walking too loudly. He'd call me "Fe-Fi-Fo-Fum." I'd laugh and say, "Okay, got it. I'm sorry."

Our differences seemed inconsequential in the grand scheme of things. I never doubted that we'd be together forever. I felt so secure about our relationship that I didn't feel any urgency to make our union official with a formal ceremony. We shopped for engagement rings, but our wedding plans never really advanced much further than that. We both had busy careers, and the demands of parenting Weslie kept our focus firmly fixed on the present.

Stephen and I both booked a Microsoft commercial, directed by our friend Jon Chu, for January 2013. For the shoot, we were dressed in business attire. Stephen wore a three-piece suit, and I was dressed in a navy blazer with a silky knee-length skirt. The script called for Stephen to jump on the table at the end of the second day of shooting and pull me up with him and dance.

The first day of shooting had been uneventful, but the second day was a whole different story. Stephen was acting cagey. He seemed nervous. I asked him a few times, "You good?" but he just mumbled incoherently. Then, to my surprise, everybody was called to the set but me. Had I done something wrong? I started to freak out. Were they not happy with my dancing? Was I being removed from the commercial? My mind was racing with a thousand possibilities, none of them pleasant. I grew more anxious at lunch, when nobody sat with me—not even Stephen. I felt completely adrift.

Frustrated and confused, I tracked down Stephen and asked him if he knew what was going on. "Don't worry," he said. "Trust me." I pressed for more details, but he just repeated, "Trust me." What did that mean?

While we were talking, my friend, dancer Jessica Lee Keller, who was also in the commercial, approached Stephen and said she needed to talk to him. I hadn't seen her all day. She took one look at me and burst into tears. Her reaction did nothing to calm my fears.

Finally, the producers came and collected me. They said I was needed on the set for the last shot of the day. I composed myself and entered a room filled with people who I was now convinced hated me. Jon instructed Stephen to hop on the table and pull me up to dance with him, as the script directed. Just as the cameras were ready to roll, an assistant rushed onto the set and said there had been some confusion with my paperwork. I couldn't be in the shot until I completed it. I was led to another room, where I sat down in front of a massive stack of papers. As I frantically filled out form after form, I realized a lot of the pages were duplicates.

The assistant insisted that I sign every last page anyway. When I was done, I was told I required touching up in hair and makeup. When I found the makeup artist in tears, I was beyond exasperated. What had started as a dream gig with my boyfriend, directed by our friend, had devolved into a nightmare.

Once I was back on the set, the music began, and Stephen hopped onto the table as directed. He pulled me up with him, and we started dancing.

Suddenly, he grabbed my hand and the music switched to Jason Mraz's "I Won't Give Up," a song that we both loved. I always found the refrain reassuring: "Well, I won't give up on us / Even if the skies get rough / I'm giving you all my love / I'm still looking up." The irony of the song title cuts me deeply now. I am still able to listen to it, but this verse makes me especially sad: "I don't wanna be someone who walks away so easily / I'm here to stay and make the difference that I can make."

As the music washed over us, Stephen whispered, "Hey, I told you to trust me." But I was barely paying attention. I was focused intently on my dancing because I saw it as my last chance to atone for whatever I had done to fall so out of favor that people were literally weeping for me.

We stopped dancing and Stephen handed me a bouquet of bird-of-paradise, my favorite flower at the time. I accepted them with a confused expression. This was not in the script. He spun me around. Standing there behind the table were my mom, dad, and Weslie. I was so confused. What were they doing here? I'd find out later that Microsoft had covered the costs of their travel, and I had been hustled out of the room to sign that mountain of paperwork so I wouldn't register their arrival on the set.

When I turned back around, Stephen was visibly shaking and sweating. "Let me try to get through this," he mumbled.

As my mind was rushing to catch up with everything that was happening, Stephen said, "Something that's always stood out to me, um, that came from a conversation I had with one of my best friends about life, accomplishments, and things of that nature, is he said the greatest accomplishment in his life was finding that one person to spend the rest of his life with. At the time, I didn't realize"—he was squeezing my right hand with his left and caressing my fingers as he spoke—"it was all work and things. I really, really understand what he means now, because out of all the places I've been and all the things I've done, you're easily my greatest inspiration. I would be honored"—he chuckled nervously as he reached for the ring in his pocket—"if I could spend the rest of my life with you. Allison Holker"—he bent down on one knee—"will you marry me?"

Oh. My. God. This was his proposal. Everyone on set was in on it—except me. How in the hell did Stephen pull it off? Jon, who had been in on the scheming from the start, looked inordinately pleased with himself. So did Stephen, who had clearly gone to so much trouble to make the moment memorable and meaningful. Having my parents there—and especially Weslie—meant everything to me.

Of course I said yes. First I nodded my assent, and then I shouted it. "YES!" The rest is a blur. I challenge anyone to come up with a weirder, wilder, more wonderful engagement story.

We set our wedding date for later in the year: December 10. We were both hustling, taking every job that came our way. We were cobbling together perfectly respectable careers, but we had more fame than fortune. We'd never been busier. But if you looked at our bank accounts, you'd have thought we were running in place. Childcare costs ate up a significant chunk of my earnings. We were both making good money but not big money, which is all to say that we weren't sure how we were going to afford a wedding with at least two hundred guests.

Enter Nigel Lythgoe, one of the creators of *So You Think You Can Dance*. Nigel had seen us grow individually and as a couple. He has always been supportive, and he generously offered to host our wedding at his 164-acre Tuscan-style vineyard in Paso Robles on the Central Coast, midway between San Francisco and Los Angeles. Named Villa San Juliette, it's an incredibly romantic setting, with sick views of the vineyards, which sit atop the earth like braids atop a skull, for as far as the eye can see.

As soon as we toured the castle-like grounds, we knew it was just right. We resumed our busy lives and got totally wrapped up in work.

Around October, with the wedding eight weeks away, my dear friend Travis called to ask if we were still planning to get married in December. "Yes," I said brightly. "Why do you ask?" Travis explained that he hadn't received his save-the-date card or an invitation. Right. Invitations. Somehow, we had overlooked that minor detail on our daily to-do lists.

Thank goodness I had a friend, Troy Williams, who planned red-carpet events. He was happy to jump in and take over the organizing of our wedding. I told him my main concern was not the color scheme or flowers or even my dress. I wanted to make sure we had a great dance floor for the reception.

Who knew that my main concern should have been the weather? The day before our wedding, it was bitterly cold, and not just cold for California. It actually snowed. There was some concern that we might have to move the ceremony indoors to a church. But when the idea was presented to us, we were united in our desire to stay the course. Our wedding day dawned cold, but none of our guests were heard complaining.

Never ones to stand on tradition, Stephen and I decided to stay in the same room the night before our wedding. We didn't want to be separated, and it was exciting to wake up next to each other on our big day. We had decided to write our own vows, and Stephen, to stiff-arm his social anxiety, had written his words well in advance of the wedding and practiced his delivery daily. I wrote mine in a notebook on the way to the venue as Stephen drove and Weslie sat in the back. The loving energy inside the car provided the perfect inspiration, and the deadline pressure brought out my best work. Our wedding party consisted of ten groomsmen and ten bridesmaids. God bless every last one of them, because far from fading out of my life over time, they've really shown up for me, especially over the past year and a half. They were there in the beginning and at the end, and I'm so, so grateful for that.

Before the ceremony, as I was waiting to walk down the grand staircase toward where Stephen and the other members of the wedding party and guests had gathered, I could hear our friend Melinda Doolittle, an *American Idol* alum and gospel singer extraordinaire, at the white grand piano, bringing down the house with her rendition of "I Won't Give Up." It was exquisite. I got goosebumps.

My bridesmaids and mom had already preceded me down the aisle, so I was all alone at the top of the staircase except for Nigel's preteen grandson, who was playing a video game. I was nervous and needed someone to talk to. The kid would have to do.

"I'm about to get married," I told him. "If you could give me any advice, what would you say?"

He considered my question. "Well, you seem happy," he said. "Are you happy?"

"Of course," I replied.

"Then that's all you need to know," he said with a shrug.

It was such a perfect response, one that still gives me chills. From the mouths of babes. Nigel's grandson gave me the best advice—not only for that moment but for my life in general. If you lead with light, you'll always be headed in the right direction.

As soon as I descended the staircase, I noticed that I had my own personal paparazzo snapping photographs. It was Nigel, and he was totally into it. I met up with my dad, who was visibly shaking from nerves. I calmed him down by saying, "We have this. It's okay." It was funny. I mean, wasn't that supposed to be his line?

We turned the corner and I saw all our guests, most of them crying happy tears. And then I saw Stephen. I'll never forget his expression. It was so sweet and pure. When I reached the end of the aisle and locked eyes with him, he grabbed my hand and pulled me in for a kiss. I was like, *No! We have to wait!*

Stephen said his vows first, and he was as nervous as the day he proposed. He let everyone know that he had forgotten everything he wanted to say—so much for all that practicing he did—which made everyone laugh. I might have laughed the loudest, since I had suggested he bring his notes and he had brushed me off, insisting that he'd remember what he wanted to say.

"Allison, you are my champion of champions," he began. "You are beautiful, kind, special, creative, and incredibly loving. You have such an incredible life force that drives you, and it affects everyone you encounter.

"From the moment we met I knew something in my life was about to change. At the time, the word *change* scared me. I'm a creature of habit and I was free to create my habits alone. What could be better than what I had then? The missing link: love and family. You went on to show me that you would be there by my side to walk with me through challenges, fears, good times and bad. I was afraid that I was not ready to be the champion you and Weslie need, but you have awoken the best part of me. And as life goes on, you continue to show me things about myself that I don't believe I could achieve alone. Some processes have been easier and some very challenging. But that's the beautiful thing about a life of love.

"I lovingly accept these challenges to help our love for each other, our children, and the rest of the world grow. I accept the challenge every day to be a better friend, lover, husband, and father. I pledge to you endless strength you can count on when you are weak. I'll be your music when you can't hear, your sunshine when you can't see, and your perfume when you can't smell. You'll never need to look further than me. I'll be your spark of light in the darkness and your hope when you're down and out. I'll be by your side forever."

I had Weslie standing sweetly by my side blessing the union and my notes in my hand so I wouldn't leave anything out. "Stephen," I said, "from the moment we locked eyes, I knew we shared something special. And that feeling is still so strong. You brought a happiness, a love, and security to our family, and I am forever grateful that you made that leap into my life and the life of my daughter.

"There is a special light inside you, and it transcends through the whole wide world, so bright, and you have brought that same light out of me and Weslie. Every day we grow together, every day is ever changing, every day brings a new obstacle, but I am brave when I'm at your side. Having your support has made me a stronger person.

"We are about to embark on this huge journey, Stephen, and we don't know what lies ahead, but what I do know is that I have you. And with you, I, you, our family . . . we can conquer anything. And with having a strong, humble, courageous man, I promise you I will try every day to work on being a strong counterpart, an even stronger friend, and the best wife I can be. I will be fearless, I will be an ear, I will be your biggest supporter, and I will give you the love that you deserve.

"I, Allison, take you, Stephen, to be my husband, my partner for life, and my one true love. I will cherish our union and love you more each day than I did the day before. I will trust you, respect you, laugh with you, and cry through the good days and the bad. Stephen, I give you my hand, my heart, and all of my love."

We received a congratulatory card that pretty much distilled my message to its essence: *To have and to hold until we're really, really old.*

The reception turned into an amazing dance party. We didn't think we could afford the fancy light-up dance floor that was our heart's desire. But Troy, bless him, made it happen. It was his gift to us. We were ecstatic. Everyone in our wedding party got to choose their walk-up music for the dance floor. Stephen and I made our entrance to Color Me Badd's "I Wanna Sex You Up," and I thought our grandparents were going to topple out of their chairs. Travis Wall and Will Wingfield, a contemporary dancer who placed in the top eight in Season 4 of *So You Think You Can Dance*, made their entrance to The Weather Girls's "It's Raining Men," holding umbrellas and my veil. It was awesome!

The dancing was fantastic, and it allowed our families to blend seamlessly. The room lit up as everyone got their groove on. You could literally feel the love in the air. It was like a tamer version of the Federal's dance floor, populated with professional dancers from *So You Think You Can Dance*, *Dancing with the Stars*, the *Step Up* movies, and more. There were so many tremendous dancers but not a single ego—just unfiltered joy. It was the most incredible party I've ever experienced, the dance version of a Thanksgiving potluck featuring all your favorite professional chefs from the Food Network.

During the reception, Stephen, Weslie, and I did a dance together. Five-year-old Weslie had choreographed it, and we had first performed it at her school. She wanted to showcase it at the wedding, and it became one of my favorite moments. She was so shy at the time, she'd typically hide behind my leg when people wanted to talk to her. So for her to get out there and perform was a big deal, and we were very proud of her. Stephen also had a dance with his mom, and I had a dance with my dad. What I didn't anticipate was each of my brothers stepping in to take a turn to dance with me, which were truly special moments.

Later in the evening, we danced to our song, "One and Only" by Adele. We didn't care that it stretches nearly six minutes. In each other's arms, the time flew by.

All our worries about the logistics were for naught. The day was perfect from beginning to end. We were so happy to be heading into our happily ever after. We had grand plans, both professionally and personally, for our lives together.

CHAPTER 7

PUSH IT REAL GOOD

Soon after our wedding, Stephen and I began talking about expanding our family. I love, love, love kids, and we knew we wanted more children. Stephen had expressed to me, and many others, that he wanted a large family: his own basketball team of Bosses, ideally. Or, as he described it, "a whole tribe." Easy for him to say! His body didn't have to contain and cultivate each member for up to forty weeks. A dance career is not indefinite, and neither is the window for having children. Given that my moneymaking abilities revolved around the instrument that is my body, the complexities of the conversation became obvious. And not long after our wedding, our work lives became exponentially busier. There was no shortage of work.

I was collaborating on a semi-regular basis with Derek Hough on choreography for *Dancing with the Stars*. In 2013, the same year Stephen and I were married, I was nominated with Derek for an Outstanding Choreography Emmy for our work on two pieces, and I was a featured dancer in two other nominated pieces.

Stephen was also keeping busy with his own projects. But something about us being a married couple caused our careers to shift into overdrive as we also became attractive to prospective employers as a package deal. We were both totally cool with working together as long as we were compensated equally and could continue to pursue individual projects.

No collaboration would have been bigger or meant more to either of us than creating children. Stephen would have had me pregnant every year of our marriage if it were up to him. I was like, *Whoa, not so fast! Let's enjoy each other's company for a while and love on Weslie, shall we? Everything in its own time.* We went with the flow and let the universe work its magic.

Even though it was true that my body was the one that would carry a child, I was not deterred by how a pregnancy might complicate my career. I've always been determined to do it all. I only get this one life, and I want it to be as big as I can make it. I'm not going to follow anybody's designs on how to construct it. (Weslie is proof of that.) There is no perfect timeline. Life is imperfect and complicated no matter how much you might try to exert control over it, so if you want to have kids and a career, my attitude has always been to go for it. Don't hold back! For me, being a mother and having a career and traveling the world isn't complicated; it's . . . life.

I was never shy about taking on new adventures, which is how I came to branch out into choreography for music videos and other projects. I was in demand for dancing workshops and masterclasses. I did backup dancing for Demi Lovato, Rihanna, and Pitbull and for *The X Factor USA*, a singing-centric show created by Simon Cowell.

I danced with Demi for a few months beginning in November 2011, mostly at festivals and fairs as she prepared to head overseas for her first world tour in early 2012. My protective instincts went into overdrive around her. She was so freaking talented and under so much pressure, as headline performers of any age invariably are. I wanted to be there for her as long as I could. But I passed on the full US tour and international dates because I couldn't be there for Demi and my daughter, too, and my first responsibility was to Weslie.

In 2013, a few months after we became engaged, Stephen and I performed together on *Dancing with the Stars* to "Crystallize," accompanied on the violin by the amazing Lindsey Stirling. When I talk about us getting more work opportunities as a couple, this is what I mean.

When the producers invited me to a meeting in 2014, I assumed they were interested in my choreography skills. Instead, they threw me a curveball by offering me an opportunity I'd never dreamed of: They asked me to join the twelve cast members as a pro dancer for Season 19.

They knew what I could do choreography-wise because of my previous work with Derek. Still, the fact that I wasn't ballroom-trained was a big deal. No way would I have let that minor detail preclude me from taking on such an exciting challenge. I told them of course I knew how to ballroom dance! I figured that if I put my mind to it, I could get up to speed quickly.

My participation on the show was not universally embraced. I received some snubs from the other pros because I didn't come from their ballroom world. But the added pressure made me better because it forced me to work that much harder. I needed that push. I had a few brutal moments, which is to be expected given there were some dances I did that first season that I had never attempted before. The very first quickstep I ever did in my life was on the biggest ballroom show that exists—and I had to pick the song, choreograph it, and teach someone else how to do it on top of learning how to do it myself. It was wild! I had never done a paso doble, a rumba, a Viennese waltz. I was figuring them out in real time, with one week to learn the steps and choreograph a routine. I turned to ballroom dance sites on the internet to research different steps and moves.

I was determined to acquit myself well. I watched all the playback videos and absorbed all the feedback. I got better. I had to find the right balance between satisfying the judges but also bringing my own flair and energy to the dances. There were a couple moves that are usually done in one particular direction because of how the partnering hold works—a windmill move with my arms quickly comes to mind—and I was like, *Why not? I'm going to do it.*

Ballroom dancing has an amazing electric energy that I love so much.

When you're a jazz dancer or a ballet dancer, you learn how to be part of an ensemble. You have to be a team player. Ballroom is for the most part a solo act, even as part of a pair. Every time you walk onto the floor, your goal is to get every eye on you. In a competition, there may be twenty or thirty couples on the floor at the same time doing different routines to the same music, and everyone is performing to get the judges' attention in a way that screams, "*Look at me!*" If you're just blending in, you're never going to win.

In that respect, ballroom greatly improved my stage presence. It taught me how to own the room and own my power. Before I was on the show, when I'd walk into a space, people might notice me but I wasn't trying to get their attention. I was content to be another dancer in the room. But ballroom conditions you to carry yourself with an attitude of *You will pick me.* It taught me not to be scared of wanting (and getting) all eyes on me. Even costume-wise, I became bolder. Thanks to the show, I've bought tons of rhinestone outfits, and I'm not scared to wear them to the grocery store or to the park with my kids.

Another thing about ballroom dancing not a lot of outsiders get is that chemistry is more important than any of the dance steps or choreography. You have to develop a connection with your partner, and it's not a given that that will happen. It's not something that can be faked. If they're not comfortable with you, none of the beautiful choreography you create will matter. To create chemistry requires being open and vulnerable, which isn't easy. As the professional in the pair, I'm not just the teacher or the trainer. I'm a kind of psychologist, almost a mother figure. I was fortunate to have really lovely partners who worked hard and were patient with the fact that I was an actual working mother, with time constraints and responsibilities that my single partners didn't have.

In my debut in fall 2014, I partnered with *Mean Girls* actor Jonathan Bennett. He made me laugh in every single rehearsal. It was hard to be stressed when I was holding my sides until they hurt—and not from any of our dancing moves. Nothing seemed to bother Jonathan. Our jazz performance was accompanied by pyrotechnics, including a smoke machine that was so loud we couldn't hear the start of our music. We looked at each other as if to say, *What do we do?* We started our routines a few seconds late—it seemed like an eternity—but Jonathan just rolled with it. He was a trouper, and we had a blast. We were eliminated in Week 6, finishing in ninth place.

The next season I partnered with the singer and actor Riker Lynch, who was an amazing dancer—seriously. I threw routines at him that were crazy hard; even seasoned pros would have struggled to learn them. I warned him that I was going to create killer choreography for him because he was so good, and he was game for it all. He worked extraordinarily hard and picked up the moves quickly. He really wanted to be great. (On a side note, Riker put almost as much time and effort into his hair as he did his dancing, and I mean that as a compliment. I idolized him for it! I took notes because I wanted my hair to look just as fabulous.)

The choreography for our paso doble dance was one of the routines that I'm the most proud of to this day. It's my favorite piece of choreography, in no small part because of its backstory. We were originally assigned to perform to music from Disney's *Toy Story*, which was *so* not us. Riker and I are both obsessed with *Pirates of the Caribbean*, so I asked if we could dance to something from that instead. "No go," I was told. "*Pirates of the Caribbean* has not been approved. *Toy Story* has been approved. Ergo, you will dance to *Toy Story*."

I stood my ground. I understood that it was expensive to get music approved, but I had a killer vision for *Pirates of the Caribbean*, and I trusted my instincts. I fought for it. I began to choreograph a routine to *Pirates* without having gained approval. I taught Riker the piece in two days, and we recorded a video of us performing it that I sent to the producers to show the people at Disney. It was a risky proposition on my part. Thank goodness they loved the piece and approved the music; otherwise, I would have had to choreograph something completely new on the fly for *Toy Story*.

We advanced all the way to the finals, finishing second behind Rumer Willis and her pro partner, Valentin Chmerkovskiy. Riker and I kept in touch afterward—he even hired me for one of his music videos. My favorite part of the *Dancing with the Stars* experience really is the friendships that I've made.

I returned for Season 21 and finished seventh while paired with the singer Andy Grammer. While rehearsing with Andy in late summer 2015, I looked at myself in the mirror and I just knew—*I'm pregnant*. Brimming with excitement and curiosity, I took a pregnancy test. When it came up positive, I couldn't wait to share the news with Stephen, who was also in rehearsals on the same lot for *So You Think You Can Dance*.

I sprinted across the lot to find him and burst into his rehearsal, no doubt appearing a bit frantic. I asked if we could step outside to talk, and in the alley behind the rehearsal rooms I blurted, "I'm pregnant! We're having a baby!"

Stephen's face lit up with joy. We hugged and hopped around like little kids, overwhelmed with happiness. I had to tell him to compose himself before he returned to rehearsal because we had to keep the news to ourselves until I got past the first trimester.

Stephen deserved an Oscar nomination for how well he acted as if nothing was out of the ordinary. When the time came to announce the pregnancy to the world, we chose to do it during an episode of *Dancing with the Stars*. It was Most Memorable Week, where participants dance to celebrate a special time in their lives. Erin Andrews, who was interviewing Andy and me, turned her attention to Stephen and Weslie, who joined us on camera. I wore a royal blue halter-style leotard with strategic rhinestone cutouts that concealed my tiny bump. I revealed the exciting news. It was a moment that will forever be etched in my memory.

Andy sweetly commented that we were now a dancing trio—him, me, and the baby made three. He was so patient and kind. He proved to be an excellent partner for me. The dancing experience during my second pregnancy was in stark contrast to my first, where I had to conceal Weslie's existence due to the harsh judgments of people with biases against working mothers. This time I was surrounded by unwavering support. I was the first woman in the history of *Dancing with the Stars* to compete while pregnant, and my condition was celebrated. Far from having to hide my pregnancy, I was encouraged to proudly showcase my baby bump in fitted leotards and shimmering costumes. At four-and-a-half-months pregnant, I was flaunting my condition in these itty-bitty outfits. I had to make frequent trips to the bathroom to pee, and each time I needed three people to help me peel the outfit off and put it back on. It was wild but worth every minute.

Did my baby bump set off a baby boom in the professional dance world? It sure felt like it. In the half dozen years following my season as a pregnant pro, several other *DWTS* pros had babies, including Lindsay Arnold, Sharna Burgess, Witney Carson, Jenna Johnson, Kym Johnson (who had twins!), Daniella Karagach, Peta Murgatroyd, and Karina Smirnoff. All of them received widespread support from network officials, fellow dancers, and the public after announcing their pregnancies. It made this mama proud to see the strides the industry had made in accepting dancing moms.

In 2024, when I served as a judge alongside Maksim Chmerkovskiy, he told me that my dancing while pregnant and then as a mom gave him and his wife, Peta, the inspiration they needed to go ahead and start their family without fearing it would negatively impact their careers. It was nice of Maks to say that. This shift in attitude in the lifetime of my sixteen-year-old daughter Weslie is something I'm gratified to have contributed to. Nobody should face the ostracism that I did during my pregnancy with her.

Being on *Dancing with the Stars* while pregnant truly became a family affair. It wasn't just me up there; it was me and my baby. And Stephen and Weslie never missed a show. It was such a wonderful time in our lives. We were incredibly grateful and ecstatic.

During filming, with our expanding family in mind, Stephen and I bought our first detached home together, in Encino. It was madness juggling two careers, the demands of one small child with another on the way, moving, and, oh, did I mention I accompanied Andy on his iHeartRadio tour in between tapings so that we could practice in between shows? We were on a plane almost every night, returning to LA for dress rehearsals and to film, and then it was back on the road.

Stephen and I somehow balanced this schedule, and we made sure it worked for Weslie too. It helped that both Stephen and I seemed to thrive in chaos. The busier we were, the better we managed. We shared the "Let's go for it" mantra, which is why we worked so well together.

In addition to choreographing my dances with Andy, I decided that it would be neat to organize a flash mob dance for Stephen for our gender reveal. It was an elaborate setup, involving seventy-five people, a group of Australian tourists who happened upon the scene, and a mariachi band. I had a seven-minute routine in mind, but it was a bear to organize since Stephen and I were around each other all the time. I rented a studio space near one of our favorite restaurants, and on the appointed day, I asked Stephen to meet me there at noon for lunch.

Two hours before our lunch, I gathered all the dancers in the studio to learn the choreography for the dance only to have Stephen text to say he was on his way—forty-five minutes early! I threw my hands in the air and basically told everybody to improvise and have fun with it. We were spread out over several blocks. I had invited my parents and Stephen's mom, so they were there too.

Stephen approached the restaurant and saw my dad and hesitantly waved at him, like he wasn't sure if what he was seeing was real or an apparition. I grabbed him by the arm and said, "Hey, baby, let's go." I helped him slip on a jacket that I had miked up and added, "Walk with me." We passed all the dancers, who were giving it their all. At the end of the road, so to speak, stood his mom, Weslie, and my mom, who opened up their jackets to reveal shirts that read "It's a Boy."

Our baby boy, as it turned out, really enjoyed his time in my belly. Even at two weeks past his due date, he seemed in no hurry to vacate my womb. I resorted to all the tricks to induce labor, including eating extremely spicy food and climbing stairs morning, noon, and night. But our little boy was stubborn. We discussed inducing labor or having a cesarean section, and I wasn't opposed to either option, but having experienced natural childbirth before, I trusted my body to handle it. I had a feeling our son would join us when he was good and ready.

Stephen and I had planned a lavish Easter barbecue at our house, anticipating that we'd be celebrating Jesus' resurrection *and* our son's birth. (I repeat: We plan. God laughs.) We invited both our families and a ton of friends. It was the first party at our new place, so we spared no expense. We went all out with decorations and bunny cupcakes—the whole nine yards. Weslie even set up a lemonade stand to sell drinks. The party was in full swing when I realized I was in labor. The contractions started coming strong, about every minute or two. I grabbed Stephen, who immediately spun into a mini panic. He was going around in circles as his mind raced with questions, the main one of which was *What do we do now?*

I chose that moment to grab a hamburger for a quick snack. I thought Stephen was going to lose his everlasting mind. Hey, a girl's gotta eat, amirite? I had complete confidence that my body knew what it was doing, and I hoped that by exuding calm, my composure would rub off on Stephen. I didn't feel too bad, just a tad uncomfortable, so I continued to circulate and check in with our guests to see how everyone was enjoying the party. I sat down to eat my burger, and that's when my body convulsed with excruciating pain. I squeezed Stephen's leg hard, grunting, "No. No. No."

It was go time. We didn't want to cause a panic, so Stephen quietly asked if I could stand up. I couldn't without his help. We made an announcement that we were headed to the hospital but encouraged everybody to stay and have fun. We'd be back soon!

We needed to get to UCLA Medical Center, which could take anywhere from thirty minutes to over an hour, depending on LA traffic. With Stephen driving and Weslie excitedly jabbering away in the back seat, we made good time. I informed the nurses that my first labor had taken four hours, so my doctor needed to be summoned immediately. They checked me in and discovered that I wasn't kidding. I was very dilated, at the edge of no longer being able to get an epidural.

It became a race against the clock. For a baby who took his sweet time coming into the world, he wasn't fooling around now. Stephen knew his role. He put on the playlist that we had curated for the occasion—jams from J. Cole, Kendrick Lamar, Jay-Z, and other hip-hop artists. We were singing along to the beats to calm our nerves. Nurses would pop their heads in to see who was playing such hardcore music. They explained that mothers typically opt for classical or calming tunes during labor. Instead, we were getting down to Lil Jon & The East Side Boyz's "Get Low": "Three, six, nine, damn she fine / Hopin' she can sock it to me one more time / . . . To the window (Give dem di dance now), to the wall (To the wall) . . ."

My doctor finally arrived, did a cursory examination, and said, "Let's do this." I began with some practice pushes, using the breathing techniques I'd learned with Stephen in our birthing classes. Those classes, by the way, were hilarious. We did our best to add levity to the proceedings by asking uncomfortable questions to make the other couples laugh. On occasion the last laugh was on us as Stephen would fall asleep. But when it mattered, his training kicked in, and an alert Stephen shuffled our playlist so that Salt-N-Pepa's "Push It!" filled the room. The party was *on*.

My doctor stood in position, surrounded by four nurses, with Stephen and my mother also front and center. Everyone, even my prim and proper mother, was singing "Push It!" I was laughing so hard. I had an entire choir singing, "(Push it) / Push it real good!" My doctor yelled, "Keep laughing! It's working!" And that's how Maddox made his grand entrance on March 27, 2016. My Aries baby weighed in at eight pounds, fifteen ounces, and measured twenty-two inches.

A week later, Stephen and I posted photos to our Instagram pages of Maddox's tiny fingers gripping Stephen's right index finger. He wrote: "'She can make angels, I've seen it with my own eyes . . .' Allison you never cease to amaze me. I love you and thank you for bringing in our little angel so gracefully. Seriously, I fall in love with you over and over again because you are such a champion."

Being a family of four created a wonderful dynamic. Stephen, Weslie, and I were already a tight unit, and making room for Maddox was surprisingly easy. He radiated joy and lit up our household. He brought a new level of happiness and vibrancy to our world. Maddox hit all his milestones—crawling, talking, and walking—earlier than most babies. At a few months old he was already jamming to hip-hop music and showed a lot of rhythm. But then, he had entered the world to "Push It!" What did we expect? Like the rest of us, he was always on the go and ready for new adventures.

We had initially wondered how we'd juggle Weslie's school and extracurricular activities and our demanding jobs with caring for a newborn. But with a little help from our friends and family, it all fell into place. If I got tired in the middle of a meeting, Stephen would take over. If he said that he had a big workday ahead, I'd offer to look after the kids. Like any parents, we were overwhelmed at times, but we never hesitated to bring Maddox and Weslie along with us to work. I cherished feeding the baby on set and having the kids watch our rehearsals. We wanted them to be a part of the life we were creating for them.

In 2014, Stephen accepted a job on *The Ellen DeGeneres Show* as the hype person responsible for energizing the studio audience and keeping them entertained during lulls in the filming. It was a spotlight-adjacent role, but as time went on, Stephen's effervescent personality rose to the fore like so many champagne bubbles. He took on the duties of house deejay. While he had grander ambitions—including one day hosting his own show—he embraced the persona and became Ellen's winsome sidekick.

I'd regularly hear from people who told me that they tuned in to watch expressly to see Stephen. He spent nearly a decade by Ellen's side and experienced genuine happiness as part of Ellen's showbiz family. He found the atmosphere filled with love and positive energy, and he was genuinely fond of Ellen. I have many lovely memories of collecting Weslie from school and Maddox from preschool and driving to the studio to watch the taping of the show. The kids would sneak snacks from the greenroom and get so excited to see Stephen on the stage. Everyone affiliated with the show became like our second family.

A few months after Maddox was born, I returned for Season 23 of *Dancing with the Stars*. I wasn't immediately told who I'd be paired with. Instead, I was given an address and told to show up there to meet my dance partner. The location turned out to be a music studio. Walking down the hallway, I took in the gold and platinum records lining the walls on either side and I was like, *Oh my God! Oh my God!*

At the end of the hallway I discovered . . . the singer-songwriter Kenneth "Babyface" Edmonds. Babyface extended my run of luck with partners. I could not have wished for a better one. He was such a gentle soul. From him, I learned so much about dedication, creativity, and never giving up on your artistic visions.

The thing I liked the most about Babyface is that he's not only one of the most celebrated R&B artists but also the central character in the R&B video that is his life—and he never breaks character. He lives and breathes rhythm and blues. He's quiet, but his energy is loud. The first day we met, he started writing as I was sitting there with him, and in ten minutes he had composed lyrics to a beautiful song.

We were eliminated in Week 4 and finished in eleventh place, but that was just the beginning of our friendship. His kids and mine have gone trick-or-treating together. A more solid citizen you will not find. Partners like Babyface made my time on *DWTS* memorable, but I gained so much more than friends during my time on the show. It was an invaluable experience for my career. As a pro, I essentially filled the roles of lighting director, costume director, artistic director, music director, choreographer, and performer. I was learning all these new skills on the fly, under duress, and I loved every second.

Despite the long hours and stress of our jobs, Stephen and I made a concerted effort not to let our work spill over into our personal lives. Our time together with our kids was filled with fun.

We were thrilled when we were approached about hosting the holiday special *Disney's Fairy Tale Weddings: Holiday Magic*, directed by Simon Lythgoe, the son of our dear friend Nigel at whose vineyard property we had wed. We also hosted a season of the series *Disney's Fairy Tale*

Weddings. Our wedding had been a fairy tale, so it was a supreme honor to be part of other people's once-in-a-lifetime moments. You couldn't have asked for a more alluring assignment. Our roles were to draw back the curtain on weddings and engagements at Disney destinations around the world. We were part of one proposal on top of a glacier during a Disney Alaskan cruise. We witnessed another that took place underwater during a different cruise. I'm not surprised that our social media following spiked through our exposure on the show because it was a magical premise, executed beautifully.

The shooting days tended to be long because we had to film around Disney's regularly scheduled activities at its various properties. What I hadn't known until we did this show is how much cleaning and sprucing up happens at the Disney theme parks after hours. It wasn't unusual to have to wait until three in the morning to shoot a wedding at the Sleeping Beauty castle.

A show centered around proposals and weddings didn't seem like the right place to announce a pregnancy. It seemed a little presumptuous. But we were expecting again. We made the surprise announcement that I was carrying my third child on the 2019 Mother's Day episode of *The Ellen DeGeneres Show.* I remember Ellen playfully chiding Stephen, saying, "How long have you known and kept this from me?" Stephen replied, "It's been a while, Ellen. It's been a little while. But you know, we gotta keep it under wraps for a second."

I was pregnant with Zaia during the filming of *Disney's Fairy Tale Weddings,* and I'm not going to lie, there were times toward the end of a long day when I'd look at Stephen and joke, "I might have this baby tonight." I was on my feet for so many hours. I'm usually a tough cookie, but I remember one night my legs felt so rubbery from fatigue that I could hardly stand. At one point in the scene, you can actually see Stephen physically holding me up. He had his arm around me, bracing me.

With this new life growing inside me, the time felt right to take a step back from dance and consider what other paths I might explore. I was ready to go in a different direction, engage in something less demanding of my time and body. I love being onstage, but my focus was shifting to producing, hosting, and brand work. Stephen was at the point where he really enjoyed acting—more so than dancing—and we took meetings for an afternoon talk show that I would produce and Stephen would host (if he had his way, with me by his side as cohost).

Envisioning what I'd like to tackle next in my career, I refused to limit myself to the world of dance. It'll always be a part of my life, but I was eager to test new muscles. Home design has always been a passion of mine, so much so that I'd binge-watch shows on HGTV. It was an area I decided to explore. I began looking for investment properties to buy and breathe new life into. It might seem as if I was veering wildly out of my lane, but I see a lot of similarities between home design and dance. Both are about storytelling. Designing a home is very much like choreographing a routine: What emotions do you want to evoke? What do you want someone to feel when they are watching a performance or moving through a room? How do you want them to feel after you take your last step in a routine or they walk out the front door?

I looked forward to showcasing this other side of my personality. When I was immersed in the twenty-hour days of dance shows, I had little time or energy to devote to cooking, design, homemaking, and crafting—all things that help transform a house into a home. It took a while to realize my dream of hosting a show on HGTV, but eventually it became a reality with a competition series called *Design Star: Next Gen*.

A revival of a successful older series on the network, the show, which featured eight designers/renovators completing an array of challenges in a bid for their own HGTV show, was filmed during the pandemic. It aired in 2021 and 2022, with Stephen serving as a guest judge for one episode. It was a fantastic experience. I had more projects with HGTV in the pipeline, but as of August 2024, that's where they remain: not dead, but not a done deal.

Not surprisingly, I danced the night before I went into labor with Zaia. Stephen and I posted the video on social media without knowing I was about to give birth. Those patio dances, as we called them, were a joy.

They represent some of my happiest moments. Since it was November, my mom and I went shopping for holiday decorations at HomeGoods. (I was eager to avail myself of her employee discount.) We were in the long checkout line with our two carts of stuff, including a couple of super cute Christmas gnomes that I had stumbled upon, when I suddenly felt those telltale pangs.

I looked at my mom and said, "Oh, no. No. No. No. Here we go again."

"Should we go?" Mom asked.

"No. No. No. No. I can make it," I assured her. I figured I had some time.

I called Stephen to let him know what was happening. "Put those carts away and come home!" Stephen said. I could tell he was in freak-out mode.

But any HomeGoods shopper knows that if you leave your treasures behind, they're going to be gone when you return. No way was I leaving without my Christmas gnomes! Keeping my voice as calm as possible, I told Stephen to pick up Weslie at soccer practice and I'd meet him at home.

Mom and I got home with the gnomes to find Stephen and Weslie frantically packing for me. I sat there unfazed, watching everyone running around in circles, throwing anything they thought I might need in the suitcase. Finally, I yelled to Stephen, "Time to go." We hurried to the car and Stephen raced toward UCLA Medical Center. My contractions were one minute apart. I thought Stephen might have to deliver the baby on the shoulder of the 405 or on the side of Sepulveda Boulevard—no joke. It was a close call, but we made it. By then, my labor was so advanced that I had to be wheeled into the hospital.

The nurses wanted to check me in before they called my doctor. I instructed them to call the doctor immediately because this baby was definitely on its way. My doctor rushed in, and before I was fully reclined, Zaia LaRae slid out as if she were at a water park. The date was November 6, 2019, and Zaia weighed nine pounds, three ounces and measured twenty-one inches.

As they've grown older, I've noticed that each child's personality reflects how they came into the world. Weslie is wise, sensitive, and soulful. Maddox is silly, always laughing and dancing. Zaia is determined, independent, and fearless. She was just sixteen months old when she ended up in a leg cast after a mishap on a slide at the neighborhood park.

Zaia and I spent only her first night in the hospital. Weslie had a big event the next day at her junior high, a mock trial in which she had been cast as a lawyer. With the doctor's permission, Zaia and I left the morning after her birth. I attended the event in a suit and heels, pushing newborn Zaia in a stroller, surprising the other parents who couldn't believe I had had a baby less than twenty-four hours earlier.

Stephen and I reveled in parenthood. We set up obstacle courses for the kids in our backyard and organized our own *American Ninja Warrior* competitions. We even gave out awards. Our hope was to foster a love of physical movement, of taking on challenges.

Our family felt complete, but that didn't stop Stephen from entertaining the notion of having more kids. On the set of Jennifer Hudson's talk show on November 17, 2022, I said that I would love to start trying for another baby and Stephen agreed. "I love the little babies," he said. "I love them."

He also talked about watching *Trolls* with the kids and playing *Just Dance*, a motion-based video game, with them. "It's fun to have dance as a way for us to connect and express all of these emotions together," he said.

I believed him. Which is what made it so very incomprehensible when, three weeks later, he shrank our family instead of expanding it and disconnected from all of us forever.

CHAPTER 8

THE BOSS FAMILY

I 'm not proud to admit it, but there was a time when I received a shot
of serotonin whenever I heard someone say "I love your dancing!"
or "I love your family!" or "I love your relationship!" What can I
say? I blame the internet. Thank goodness my childhood predated cell
phones—I didn't buy my first one until I was sixteen—and social media,
affording me the ability to make youthful mistakes and missteps without
the world's gaze upon me.

The good news is my career arc dovetailed with the acceleration of
social media. The bad news is that my career arc dovetailed with the
acceleration of social media.

In 2004, when Facebook launched, I won my first of two major titles,
the New York City Dance Alliance's National Senior Outstanding Dancer.
In 2006, when Twitter (now X) came into being, I was riding the wave
of my *So You Think You Can Dance* debut. In 2010, Instagram became
a thing, and so did Stephen and I. And TikTok arrived the same year as
Maddox—2016—allowing me to chronicle my post-pregnancy return to
professional dance.

The timeline suggests that a good percentage of my followers have
been with me since my teenage dance days, and they're still hanging in

there with me sixteen years later. That's pretty wild. They've seen a lot, from my eighteen-year-old innocence and exuberance on *SYTYCD* to my life as a single mom to my storybook romance with Stephen to lots and lots of dancing to all manner of projects and productions—including two more kids—to . . . abject darkness.

I am so grateful for the followers who have stuck with me through thick, thin, and the unthinkable. Despite the negativity and unsociability that social media can aggrandize, I absolutely love it. The attraction goes beyond gaining followers. I genuinely enjoy sharing my craft and my messy life and connecting with the wider world.

When social media's fourth wall is broken and people approach me in public, there's an incredible energy that passes between us. I can best describe it as connection, love, and grace. Of course, there are moments when people go too far—like when strangers thought it was okay to rub my pregnant belly or when two overzealous fans literally pushed me to the ground to get closer to Stephen at a charity event. Not the best experiences, but for every couple of those I can think of fifty others that were nothing but light and love.

I've had fans share tearful moments with me. To this day, I hear from people about how my performance with Robert Roldan on the opening night of Season 7's *So You Think You Can Dance* to "Fix You" has helped them through tough times. For that reason and so many others, it's one of my most treasured moments on the stage. It might have been my most impactful moment. There are women who stopped dancing after high school and, now much older, say I inspired them to get back into classes and reconnect with their love of movement. Lately, I've also been a source of solace for those grappling with the loss of loved ones.

The comfort goes both ways. The way perfect strangers rallied behind me after Stephen's death was beautiful. It's a blessing to have a platform where I can give back to those who have supported my family, but especially over the past year and a half. The outpouring of love and prayers from people on the various platforms has been astonishing. The support has felt like angel wings on my back. I truly believe that my days and nights would have been much harder to bear without it.

The social media support has been absolutely crucial for our family's survival. But I'd be remiss if I didn't add that our social media platforms—or rather, the snippets of life we chose to display on them—probably became a stressor for Stephen toward the end. He had it in his head that we should *always* look like that perfect family, which was unrealistic.

Our family's popularity took off during the COVID-19 pandemic, which was a dark time for everybody. In retrospect, I wonder if Stephen didn't become a casualty, however indirectly, of it, because during that time he really, really leaned into tWitch. Like so many others, Stephen and I were stuck at home for most of 2020, our hectic schedules supplanted by hours of downtime. There was so much fear and confusion. We watched in horror as the death toll climbed. Everyone we knew was struggling. Tension hung in the air like a stubborn fog.

Stephen was restless. I was restless. The kids were restless. We decided to start dancing as a family to shake off some of our excess energy. We established a routine that benefited us physically, emotionally, and spiritually. Three times a week at 10 a.m. we danced. Then we took the next step. *Why not show people more of us?* we thought. *Let's bring love and joy into people's homes at a dark time.* With Hollywood shut down, we created our own content. We went live on social media and connected with families around the world through *Boss Family Workouts.*

We didn't shoot the videos as a side hustle to make money; we didn't even charge for the content. Nor did we shoot the videos to grow our social media following. No professional cameras, microphones, or special lighting were used to produce them. They were basically home videos that we posted once a week to hold ourselves accountable. That they benefited others who, like us, needed motivation to move their bodies when they felt stuck was an unexpected bonus.

The next thing we knew, people were tagging us on their own dancing posts. It was amazing. And then, when the world started to open up again,

I'd be out running errands and someone would stop me to say, "I was with you every week during the pandemic." We heard from people who said they survived the shelter-in-place edicts by watching our family thrive.

Stephen and I grew closer to our fans during this time, doubling down on our shared purpose to spread joy and light. Weslie's junior high class incorporated the videos into its PE curriculum. We couldn't have been more surprised or delighted to see this idea take off the way it did.

On occasion, I'll return to our videos from those days, scrolling through them the way you might flip through pages of a scrapbook. What stands out to me is the joy on all our faces. I can see now how the happiness we radiated might have been as big a draw as the dancing itself. A whole new audience was introduced to Stephen's luminous personality and mine. They got to know our children. Our family became a kind of counterprogramming to the dire news reports from all over the world.

I enjoyed being able to showcase different facets of myself. I shared my passion for design, featured some of our kids' favorite homemade meals, and highlighted games we played as a family. Soon, major companies like Pottery Barn, DICK's Sporting Goods, and Mattel approached us with deals to promote projects ranging from furniture and apparel to toys and food. It was an awesome experience, and the kids were thrilled to be the beneficiaries of all this free stuff. But mostly they loved having their mom and dad around day after day.

We had always been good guardians, albeit ones who were spread awfully thin. The pandemic allowed us a parenting reset. We were lucky—we managed to stay healthy, and so for us this dark period became a blessing in disguise. For the first time in our married lives, Stephen and I were both home every day. We weren't hopping on airplanes every weekend for dance conventions. We'd never had the luxury of going to the park with the kids for a few hours just to hang out, but we could do that now. Stephen was able to push Zaia on the swing.

I oversaw Maddox's kindergarten studies for three hours every day. I taught him basic addition and subtraction and how to write the letters of the alphabet. We conducted simple science experiments together. I treasure that time I had with him. I love that I can say I taught Maddox how to write his name. I'm not sure I could handle homeschooling on a permanent basis—my hat's off to those parents who can and do—but I'm eternally grateful for my trial by fire.

Our backyard grill, which had gone mostly unused except for parties, became Stephen's domain. He grilled almost every night.

We jointly decided not to continue with the dance conventions once they resumed. Instead of educating the next generation of dancers, we wanted to fully commit ourselves to our kids. It was absolutely the correct decision. That said, I miss the energy of the conventions. It invigorated me to see kids' faces light up when they mastered a piece of choreography, when they achieved a level of proficiency that they maybe had doubted they could reach. My choreography is really hard, so when a kid would get the steps, it was like, "Right on! Yes!" It was genuinely something worth celebrating. I miss teaching. But, really, I've never stopped working with the next generation. I simply turned my focus to our kids.

The time we gained by staying home was put to such precious use. Instead of dragging our kids along with us to our events or leaving them behind with nannies, we prioritized showing up for them. This was their time to occupy center stage. Time for us to step back and let them be the stars.

I'll never forget when Stephen and I both started attending Weslie's soccer games. She kept glancing over at us on the sideline. You could tell she was delighted to see us in our lawn chairs with our cooler filled with snacks and juice boxes. "*This* is what life is all about," Stephen and I said.

I do wonder if our contentment didn't come at a considerable cost to Stephen, exacerbating the imposter syndrome that was his kryptonite. As his fan base grew by leaps and bounds, he couldn't step out in public, not to go grocery shopping or to the movies or out to eat, without being complimented on how joyous he was, how loving he seemed, how much positive energy he spread to everyone. How he must have pushed himself to always come across as the person whom others saw. How exhausting it must have been for him.

As the world emerged from its COVID 19–induced hibernation, Stephen was thriving professionally. He took over hosting duties on Ellen's show when she was absent and became actively involved in content creation as a co-executive producer. He extended his reach by hosting other shows like *Clash of the Cover Bands* and guest judging alongside me on *The Real "Dirty Dancing."* He served as a judge on *World of Dance*. I judged *The Funny Dance Show*. We were both really excited about playing the parents in *The Hip Hop Nutcracker* for Disney, filmed in 2022 at Disney World. It was a particularly coveted assignment because we were playing the character roles of Mom and Dad, which closely mirrored our own love story.

One of the last videos that Stephen uploaded to his Instagram account—I uploaded it to mine, too—was of us dancing in our backyard to Alicia Keys's Christmas song "December Back 2 June." We shot it two days before he died, and we look perfectly in step and emotionally in sync as the lyrics wash over us: "Let's make it the best time in our lives, / Even when the rain is falling outside (True) / [. . .] Every season (C'mon) you'll give reason to love you (When?) / From December back to June . . ."

I can't emphasize enough that our happy moments—our joy in that and other videos that Stephen posted toward the end of his life—were genuine. Stephen was navigating a complex emotional landscape. He fluctuated between genuine happiness and profound sadness, flipping between the two as if his brain were a dimmer switch.

I remember being with Stephen in public and someone would compliment him on his generous spirit. I'd tug at his sleeve and say, "See, this is your gift. Your joyfulness, your ability to make people feel seen, is your superpower." Like so many others, I assumed it came naturally to him, that it was effortless. I didn't understand the cost until it was too late. Looking back, Stephen was a better actor than anyone ever could have imagined. His day-to-day life was a convincing performance of normalcy. It's hard for me to forgive myself for failing to see through his façade, because my obliviousness deprived him of the one safe space where he might have allowed himself to be vulnerable: with me.

CHAPTER 9

BABY, ARE YOU OKAY?

Have you ever read a book with a twist ending that catches you so off guard you reread it to see what subtle clues you might have missed the first time? Stephen's shock ending caused me to revisit the last months of his life to figure out what I might have overlooked.

In hindsight, I recognize behavior that hinted at his deteriorating mental state—irritability, insomnia, weight loss, a lack of energy, a disinterest in work and friends and fun. I've faced scrutiny from people for not having known what was going on. In my defense, one of Stephen's closest friends is a psychotherapist, and he didn't pick up on any warning signs either.

Maybe familiarity breeds blind spots. Over thirteen years, which is how long Stephen and I were together, behavioral patterns and habits can become so ingrained that you don't give them a second thought. I considered Stephen's random rules and clutter, his social anxiety and marijuana use, as parts of his multifaceted personality. If some of his issues gradually emerged or became more pronounced over time, I just chalked it up to him going through a challenging phase.

He concealed his depression so well. No one—not coworkers, not family members, not friends whom he considered brothers—had any idea of the depths of his despair. It's ironic that Stephen was the person others reached out to when they were having mental health challenges. Numerous friends confided in him about their depression and suicidal ideation. Like a human tugboat, he was able to guide them out of the treacherous channel of their minds and into a safe harbor.

Both of us had been a support person for our friends and loved ones. In 2022, someone close to me attempted to take their life. It was not their first attempt. Stephen was right there beside me during the phone conversations in which I encouraged them—coaxed them, really—to seek therapeutic help. I even offered to pay for it. We discussed before we fell asleep at night how we could best approach this person.

"How can I help them when they won't help themselves?" I'd lament.

"They're a beautiful person," Stephen would say. "They just need help."

This person would yell at me whenever we spoke, accusing me of not knowing what I was talking about. I'd feel thoroughly defeated and depleted, but Stephen would assure me that the short-term discomfort I was experiencing was necessary. My efforts, he said, would pay off in the long run. He was my rock through the whole situation. He did what he could to assist me, but he never once so much as intimated that he might be struggling in a similar fashion. Honestly, I don't understand why not. It would have been such a natural extension of these talks to say "You know, babe, I can relate to what they're going through" or "I'm kind of going through something similar."

I wonder all the time, *Why couldn't he take the advice he was encouraging me to give our loved one? Why couldn't he confide in me?* I would have done anything for him.

Like me, Stephen never wanted to burden people. My best guess is that he felt he should be happy, and the fact that he wasn't made him feel infinitely worse, as though he didn't deserve to live if he couldn't revel in his blessings. The only way I can explain it is that tWitch and Stephen were locked in mortal combat. One became the murderer and the other the victim.

How Stephen died was so incompatible with how he had lived that everybody was scrambling to make sense of it. The speculation was rampant: Was our marriage not the happy one we portrayed it to be? Was the end of *The Ellen DeGeneres Show* more destabilizing for him than anybody realized?

In May 2022, Ellen signed off on her eponymous show after nineteen seasons. I was in the studio audience for the final taping, and I teared up when she said to Stephen early on, "tWitch, one last time, dance with me." For Stephen, the end of the show was bittersweet. He was sad to leave his other "home," but at the same time he saw it as an opportunity to shed his deejay role and branch out into new, more ambitious ventures.

Would he have liked to have taken Ellen's place and become the host? One thousand percent yes, but several months of discussions with the network went nowhere. Stephen was disappointed, but in typical tWitch fashion he framed it in a positive light. Stephen seemed confident that somewhere, somehow, he'd have the opportunity to build his own team, rather than inherit Ellen's, and create a show more authentic to who *he* was.

I don't believe the end of the show was destabilizing, because he wasn't out of a job. There was no work slowdown for him. We had so many projects in the pipeline. It did, however, lead to a shift in Stephen's routine. For nine years, the show had given his days a structure and rhythm. No longer bound to a schedule, Stephen had more time to spend inside his head. The dark corners of his mind were not a healthy place for him to poke around in. The internal turmoil that he had suppressed while portraying happy-go-lucky tWitch on a daily basis started bubbling to the surface.

Stephen received a significant offer to become a permanent judge on *So You Think You Can Dance*. It was a coveted position, but he didn't seem as excited as I expected him to be. Our agent speculated that perhaps for Stephen it was all about the journey. Once he had reached his goals, he experienced a sense of emptiness. My best guess is he thought he could heal himself and find contentment through achievement, and when that didn't work—when each success didn't make him feel markedly better—it made him feel doubly worse.

He started turning down lucrative offers that he would have enthusiastically accepted in the past. In one instance, Stephen shockingly passed on a major opportunity because it conflicted with our dinner plans. *Our dinner plans.* He was slowly withdrawing into his shell.

His friends invited him on a boys' trip to Cabo San Lucas, and I encouraged him to go. His schedule was free, but he chose to stay home. When I found out he had turned them down, I got on the phone with his best friend, Robert, and said, "Leave it to me. Stephen *is* going to join you guys."

I had to all but pack his bag and push him out the door, but at the end of the day he went, and he seemed to have a wonderful time. He came back raving about how much he enjoyed hanging out with his friends. It was so beautiful to see him return rejuvenated. Stephen seemed his old self, but only for a flash.

More and more he came up with excuses or reasons not to do things he previously would have thoroughly enjoyed. I'd find out later there's a name for that: *anhedonia*, and it's a common symptom of depression.

At home, Stephen would spend hours reclining in a chair, ostensibly reading. People would see him with his nose in a book and assume he was a big reader. Only the nanny, Korinne, and I noticed something odd: He rarely turned the pages. When I went through his books after his death, many of the spines were barely cracked. It was obvious he had stopped reading most of them after only a few pages. The only explanation I can offer is the books were a convenient prop that the introverted Stephen used to discourage interactions. They signaled, *Don't bother me. I'm reading.*

During his time on Ellen's show, Stephen got home in time for dinner. It became a sacred meal, like family church. We had a little glass jar of questions, and we'd start the meal by pulling a slip of paper with a question from the jar to launch the conversation. These dinners were typically marked by laughter and lightness, but toward the end of 2022 they acquired an edge. Stephen became sterner with the kids, reprimanding them for resting their elbows on the table or not eating all their vegetables.

He was especially hard on Maddox. Stephen was known as playing the disciplinarian to my softie, but his patience grew thin and his tone more aggressive with the children, which was not like him at all. At one point, he instituted a rule that Maddox couldn't wear shorts, which was random and completely ridiculous.

I would talk to him about being so hard on Maddox. It was the one thing we would argue about. Stephen loved Maddox so much. I could never get a bead on his behavior toward the end. In Maddox, did he see himself as a child and project the shame he felt at that age onto his son? He was acting out of character, but he also was a beautiful soul and a loving father. All those things could be true at once. I wrote off his irritability as the restlessness of someone not used to having free time on his hands.

Another sign, in retrospect, was that Stephen's sleep patterns changed. When he was home, he stayed up most of the night playing video games. He'd be lucky to get four hours of sleep. I'd come downstairs in the early hours and encourage him to come to bed, but he would fight me on it. I shrugged it off, convincing myself that this was his way of decompressing after leaving a longtime job. Maybe because Stephen wasn't sleeping well at night, he started taking more midday naps. He complained of feeling fatigued and began drinking heavily, which was a new behavior.

One day I was putting on my makeup in front of our bathroom vanity ahead of an event. I glanced over at Stephen, who was curled in a fetal position on the bed, as if protecting himself. But from what? He was dressed from head to toe in black. He looked exhausted. I went over and gave him a kiss on the forehead and asked, "Are you good?"

He answered the same as always: "Yes."

His personal hygiene suffered. Stephen sweated a lot, particularly when dancing, but he started showering less. Things were getting . . . offensive. When he finally came to bed at night, I would find myself pleading with him to take a shower. At the time I thought he was too tired to properly care for himself. Now I know that neglecting self-care is another classic sign of depression.

I'll never forget a conversation we had on a family trip to Hawaii that summer. It haunts me because of what Stephen might have been telegraphing. We hiked to the highest point of the island of Maui, where we sat above the clouds and stared at the stars. It was so romantic, so beautiful. Intoxicated by our surroundings, we had the most incredible conversation about life after death. Stephen suggested there were a multiplicity of universes that we cross through like so many time zones. He hypothesized that this world is just one reality of many, that there are parallel realities that we can't comprehend.

At the time, I found what he said thought-provoking. Poetic, even. So profound was our back-and-forth on the topic, we continued it once we were back at the place where we were staying. Now, of course, I have so many questions. Was he attempting to tell me something and I wasn't paying close enough attention? Was he letting me know he'd thought about death more than I could have imagined? Did I make it too comfortable for him to broach the subject? After he died, I found two sentences in his notes app about death. He was romanticizing it, which also made me wonder how long he had been thinking about the beauty of death.

That wasn't the only odd thing about that trip. While the kids played on the beach, Stephen sat in the sand, wearing a black hoodie in the blazing sun. He remained strapped into his black backpack. He was never without that thing, lugging it around everywhere. It probably weighed well over fifty pounds and contained his iPad, laptop, journals, and books that he had grown oddly attached to. I never saw him pull out one of those journals or books, yet he insisted on keeping them close at all times.

As Stephen grew more distant and detached, that backpack took on symbolic import, like he was physically bearing the weight of his emotional burdens. A few times I approached him and asked, "Baby, are you okay?" He insisted he was fine. He said he was just chilling in his own world. *Fair enough*, I thought. *He's tired, and everyone unplugs in his or her own way.* It seemed to me that he was handling whatever was the matter. At least, that was the impression he gave off.

Maybe what tripped me up was the fact that Stephen and I prided ourselves on our healthy lifestyles. We did everything in our power to guard against the unpleasant or the unexpected. We drank lots of water, we ate healthy foods (Stephen's breakfast cereals notwithstanding), we exercised, we read our self-help books and said our affirmations. If we were asked how we were doing, we'd always say, "Fine!" Neither Stephen nor I was inclined to admit to having a bad day, to needing a hug.

Toxic positivity? We embodied it.

Stephen followed a website, commandinglife.com, that offers daily inspirational messages, many of which he shared on his Instagram page. In July 2022, he posted this one: "Be the first to give yourself some grace. Be the first to believe in your possibilities. Be the first to love and accept yourself just as you are. Be the first to forgive your mistakes and try again." Was he sending out a coded SOS?

Clearly, Stephen was searching for something. An influential person in his life had turned him on to the world of ayahuasca, a psychoactive tea used in traditional indigenous practices to treat physical and mental ailments. Lately, it has gained popularity among those seeking physical healing, spiritual enlightenment, or trauma relief. The experience, which is guided by a shaman, is known for inducing intense hallucinations, altered perceptions of reality, and deep introspection. Stephen's motivation was to confront the pressures of fatherhood, grapple with the absence of father figures in his own life, and address his feelings of abandonment. I admired his initiative. He wasn't openly discussing these issues with anyone, so the way I looked at it was, *What does he have to lose?*

He extended an invitation to me to join him on the trip, but the whole concept scared me. I'm not a fan of getting high, and I have zero interest in hallucinations or deep introspective journeys. Still, I told him if that's what he wanted to do, if he thought it would be a productive experience, go for it. So he booked the trip, engaged in a few phone conversations with the shaman, and met him shortly thereafter in Joshua Tree, about an hour outside Palm Springs.

We had watched the series *Nine Perfect Strangers* about a guru, played by Nicole Kidman, at a health and wellness center. When Stephen was contemplating the experience, the show is what came to mind. The reality was altogether different. Stephen later confessed that the shaman had to keep giving him more of the brew because he struggled to let go spiritually and emotionally. He was holding on too tightly to control and couldn't surrender to the process.

Stephen sent me a photo early the first night of a herd of deer and said it was turning out to be an incredible experience. Then he called me again and said the night had taken a really weird turn. He mentioned something about the shaman being locked in the bathroom. Instead of sticking it out, he decided to cut the trip short. A friend picked up Stephen the next morning and brought him home. During the drive, Stephen said he was disappointed that he didn't have any hallucinations after drinking the tea and that he had gone to address his anxiety and depression and the chaos in his head.

I've come to understand that the recommended duration for such experiences is three to seven days, with weeks of follow-up work supervised by the shaman. Stephen returned home after less than twelve hours and threw himself back into work. By not completing the process and not submitting to any follow-up sessions, he left himself more exposed and vulnerable than ever. I've since learned that for individuals with underlying mental health issues, ayahuasca can exacerbate deep-seated problems. It can bring those issues to a boil, if you will, if there is not close supervision. The outcome can be the opposite of the intended healing.

Stephen was never the same afterward. The energy he gave off was different. It was not so joyful, not so generous. It was like every day he woke up on the wrong side of the bed. He wasn't angry or mean to people; he just seemed agitated. Slightly off. Sometimes you'd talk to him and he'd space out. He wouldn't hear a word you said.

He never wanted to talk about what was going on. I thought we could communicate about anything, but I can see now that Stephen kept his interior life under lock and key and couldn't, or wouldn't, share the combination with anybody. He knew that people were picking up on his energy shift. More and more friends were asking him if he was okay. Weslie would also ask if he was all right. He insisted he was fine.

As I mentioned, Stephen was a regular user of marijuana. His habit was an open secret. I had never known him not to smoke daily. He'd go outside so he didn't stink up the house, but also because he was ashamed that he couldn't quit. The secretiveness of it was something that had long ago become normalized in our relationship. I was used to coming downstairs in the morning and collecting the hoodie and pants that he had taken off the night before and left on the patio furniture so that he didn't bring the weed smell inside with him.

He'd been making noises about quitting long before I knew him, as far back as college. He told a friend back then to punch him in the face if he ever smoked again—and as the story goes, he proceeded to take one right in the kisser. Since marijuana was a legal drug in California, I didn't give his habit much thought. It's so normalized in LA; almost everyone I know, it seems, smokes or pops gummies. It's as common as taking vitamins. I know a lot of people who treat weed the same way that our grandparents' generation did the five o'clock martini: as a socially acceptable and effective way to take the edge off after a long, hard day. It never occurred to me that Stephen might have a problem, because he never missed a single day of work. It wasn't as if he were slipping in any tangible way. From my vantage point, Stephen seemed okay.

What I didn't know until I surveyed our backyard security cameras was that Stephen's smoking had ratcheted up. He was smoking in the morning and at night. It's almost as if he used one strain of pot at the start of the day to become tWitch, then used another at night to come down from that persona. I had no idea that Stephen was in an almost constant state of being high. He was even sneaking out to smoke on the *Ellen* set. And to the best of my knowledge, nobody knew. He was really good at hiding it. If I had been aware of the extent of his usage, I would have gone into protector mode right away. I believe in rehab; I'd helped pay for multiple people close to me to go through it, and I would have made it happen for Stephen, no questions asked. But of course he would have had to be amenable to it, and Stephen's behavior demonstrated that he clearly didn't want my—or anybody else's—help. He went to extreme measures to make sure nobody suspected anything was amiss. My naivete about his smoking became apparent later when I went through the apps on his phone and realized he was visiting one of the handful of dispensaries in our area every night. He attempted to make it more challenging to smoke by storing his weed in our storage unit, which was miles from our house, but I suspect in retrospect that he headed there some of the times that he claimed to be going to the office.

He smoked to alleviate his anxiety. But it was counterproductive because Stephen's impaired state kept him from being completely present for his family, and that in turn stressed him out. He was there but not there, which fed his insecurities about how he was failing as a father. He loved being around the kids, but it was also his biggest trigger. I'm comfortable around children, probably because they were always underfoot in the community where I grew up. I can whip up arts and crafts projects with the same ease with which other moms can bake homemade chocolate chip cookies. If the kids made water ballons or painted with watercolors, Stephen would sit with us and be part of it, but he didn't feel like he knew how to properly contribute. He put a lot of pressure on himself to be the best dad. He always wanted life to look like the movies—or our Instagram page. He couldn't accept that parenting is imperfect and often messy and that's okay.

I suggested counseling more than once. He took my advice and attended a few sessions with a Black male therapist. Then the pandemic hit, and to the best of my knowledge they never talked again. I don't know that anybody could have gotten past Stephen's protective layers in such a short time. I was with him for thirteen years and I was never able to get him to open up about whatever it was that he carried inside him like a ticking time bomb.

Twenty-eight days before he killed himself, Stephen shared this inspirational message on his Instagram page: "You are always attracting the support and resources needed to complete your life vision. Trust that the Universe is working behind the scenes to move you closer to the fulfillment of your dreams. Don't give up; keep going. You have what it takes to succeed." Should I have read anything into that posting? Was I too preoccupied with work and the kids to notice that Stephen was unraveling? These are questions I've asked myself over and over. We had so many balls in the air, business-wise. We had TV projects in the works with Disney and HGTV and so much going on with our various brands, including pre-filmed commercials, that was already in the can. Why would he toil so hard to create all these opportunities and then not stick around to reap the rewards?

After Stephen's death, I discovered on his desk a multipage contract for a podcast to be produced by the same people who worked with Jada Pinkett Smith on *Red Table Talk*, her candid conversations about timely topics. Can you imagine Stephen sitting around the table with Jamie Foxx and Will Smith, two of his favorite guests from Ellen's show? It would have been tremendous. The negotiations were far enough along that twelve table topics had been identified. I stumbled across the list:

- Male role models from the '70s and '80s or lack of them
- The "absent Black father" trope
- The role hormones and emotions play in men's lives
- What happens to men when they become fathers
- How to be a good man without becoming a boring man
- Where's the fun part of being a father?
- Man care: how to take care of yourself without being selfish
- Parenting as a straight man vs. an LBGTQ+ man
- The stigma behind going to therapy and why it needs to change
- The intricacies of parenting biracial children
- Sex after having kids

- What sayings do we still use that are problematic, and where did they come from? E.g., man up, like a girl, wear the pants, grow a pair, boys will be boys
- Unlearning things from our upbringing and reprogramming
- The differences between raising boys and girls
- Should we raise our children gender neutral?
- Is toxic masculinity real?

I was floored to find out that Stephen was the one who had proposed the topics. He had presented them in meetings with producers as conversations he wanted to have because he said he knew people who'd find such discussions helpful. Not once did he intimate that this was subject matter that he was desperate to tackle. Not once did he say that he could relate to these themes, that he was among those who would benefit from the discussions. For whatever reason, he could never bring himself to acknowledge that he was the one who needed help. Instead, he took the whole *pitching for a friend* approach.

I was stunned, but maybe I shouldn't have been. Some of my fondest memories of my time spent with Stephen were the hours we wiled away in amicable silence writing in our respective journals or creating our own vision boards. We were self-starters. Explicitly asking others for assistance was never going to be our strong suit. I had my tough-cookie persona to protect. I don't know what was behind Stephen's opposition. Did he fear that people would consider him "crazy"? Or weak? Was he worried that his struggles, if they became public, would negatively impact his popularity and earning power? Did he mistrust the medical community? Did the adversity he faced in childhood and the racial discrimination he endured throughout his life disrupt his neural pathways in ways that prevented him from thinking rationally? The answers, I'm afraid, are buried with him.

In addition to the action figurines and hats and hoodies and sneakers and journals and books that Stephen had been collecting for years, he also started amassing in his final months an odd collection of statues. I'd come home from a job and there'd be new art sculptures scattered around the house. *Okay, he decided to start collecting art. Cool,* I'd think with a shrug. Only these pieces were not cool. They were disturbing. Many were humans either without eyes or with *x*'s where their eyes should be, or with faces that appeared to be melting or masks that were sliding off. He also started acquiring figurines of boys wearing goggles that concealed their eyes.

Stephen was free to buy whatever art that moved him, but I told him I would not be adding to those collections when his fortieth birthday rolled around in September. I hadn't been allowed to throw Stephen a birthday party in years. He wouldn't let me because of his social anxiety. He hated being the center of attention. But this was a milestone birthday, and to my surprise he agreed to a celebration. I pulled out all the stops. I flew in family and friends from out of town, invited roughly one hundred guests, and rented out a restaurant with breathtaking views of the San Fernando Valley and downtown LA.

Stephen seemed genuinely happy about the party until the night before. Then he started getting anxious. By nine o'clock the next morning, he was taking shots of cognac to calm himself. I did what I could to reassure him, as I had done so many times before when his social anxiety got the best of him. I promised to take care of him throughout the party. Despite my best efforts, Stephen looked less than comfortable. He was the person everybody at the party wanted to be like, but he couldn't see it.

He appeared to rally when I delivered my happy birthday speech, flashing me a look of pure love when I called him "the light of my life" and said, "I'm so thrilled to be celebrating this beautiful man, my husband. For real, I've never met a more inspiring human. Every day I wake up grateful to wake up next to this guy who is pushing himself to be a better husband and father and man every single day. I love you. Every single person who has ever met you loves you, and it's not just because you are cool. You are inspiring."

The way everyone erupted in applause when I was through, you would have thought the ball had just dropped in Times Square on New

Year's Eve. But was Stephen buying it? A dancer friend expressed concern after the party, saying that Stephen seemed to be speaking like someone in the throes of a midlife crisis. She said he was talking about not having accomplished as much as he should have at this point in his life. He mentioned feeling as if he were falling behind.

The friend's observation took on heightened meaning after Stephen's death. I couldn't help but wonder: Had he let me throw him this party because he knew he wouldn't live to see the new year or another birthday?

CHAPTER 10

"I LIED. I LIED. I LIED."

We returned home from our anniversary weekend on Sunday, December 11, and slipped right back into our routine. With the holidays approaching, Stephen and I decided to post a new dance every Monday until Christmas. We recorded the one to the Alicia Keys song I mentioned earlier. One of our holiday traditions was to display multiple Christmas trees, one of which was the family tree reserved for the children's handmade creations and keepsake ornaments. Maddox had been pestering Stephen, asking when we were going to decorate the tree. Stephen assured him that we would celebrate the tradition the next night after dinner.

Nothing seemed out of the ordinary. Our house was buzzing with laughter and holiday excitement. I went upstairs, read stories to the littles, listened to their prayers, and tucked them into bed. Back downstairs, Weslie and I snuggled on the couch and watched the season finale of *The White Lotus*. Stephen wasn't interested in the show, so it was just us girls. As we were settling in, I received a text from Stephen with a tree emoji. That was a common shorthand he used for the weed dispensary. "I'll be right back," he said.

Not long after he left, he called me and sounded freaked out. He said he was really high, which seemed totally out of character for him. For as long as I had known him, he had always waited until he got home to smoke. I offered to come get him, but he couldn't string a sentence together. He managed to convey that he just needed a minute to collect himself. I reiterated that I was more than happy to come pick him up, but he said he didn't even know where he was.

This was not an ordinary conversation. I'd never known him to act like this.

Smoking typically made Stephen more mellow, not paranoid. I was unsure what to do. We didn't have tracking information for each other on our phones, so I could only stay on the call with him and reassure him that everything was going to be fine.

When he arrived home, he was acting terribly strange. "I lied. I lied. I lied," he ranted.

Even as my mind was racing, I did my best to comfort him by remaining calm and offering him assurances that he was going to be okay. What did he lie about? Did he not go to the dispensary? If not, where did he go? Was he under the influence of a drug that was not marijuana? Was *he* the lie to which he was referring? I asked him questions, but he was incoherent.

I will be forever tormented by those two words: *I lied*.

In that moment, the best course of action, I decided, was for us to go to bed.

Promptly at 7:00 the next morning, per our routine, Stephen brought me a steaming cup of coffee in my usual Superman mug. I was seated at my vanity, already tending to my face and hair. The gesture was more than his first act of love of the day, as he described it. On this day, the coffee was also a peace offering. He apologized profusely for his bizarre behavior the night before. I explained how worried he had made me and asked him what lie he was talking about. He claimed not to remember saying that. He apologized again, then turned the conversation toward work.

We had a busy day ahead. We were supposed to drop off the kids at school, work out, and head to the office for a full slate of meetings. The next day we were scheduled to film a video connected to a passion project that predated the passion project that was our six-year-old. We were in discussions with major companies about partnering with us and funding the venture. I don't want to go into any details because I have hopes of someday shepherding the project into the world on my own. Suffice it to say it was a potentially huge undertaking, and we were ecstatic to be so close to seeing it reach fruition.

Zaia and I walked Maddox to school. When we returned, Stephen and Weslie were still at the house. He chatted with the nannies and our assistants before he took Weslie to school. Stephen insisted on driving her whenever his schedule permitted. As they headed out the door, I said, "See you. Love you." I didn't even say goodbye.

Those would be the last words I'd ever say to him.

As was the case most days when Stephen did the school run, he and Weslie stopped at a Starbucks so she could get a breakfast sandwich and drink. When he left her at the school drop-off zone, he told her, "I wish I could have been your Superman."

It was an odd statement, but Weslie didn't dwell on it; she dismissed it as a weird dad moment. They exchanged *I love yous* before he pulled out of the school lot. It was the last time she would see him. I can't get it out of my head that Stephen was already saying goodbye in his own way hours before he disappeared.

He didn't meet me at the gym or the office per our plan. It didn't raise any alarms; I figured he'd gotten busy and lost track of time. Stephen was still texting and communicating with members of our team, attending to last-minute details related to the next day's shoot and taking calls regarding what needed to be done.

I was preoccupied with filming content and making calls, touching base with the director and the camera crew. Stephen was also in touch with these people even though he wasn't at the office. He was still very much involved and on top of things.

When I got home mid-afternoon, I noticed Stephen's car was in the driveway. I went upstairs and showered. My beauty routine was more extensive than usual because of the shoot the next day and included shaving, exfoliating, and applying self-tanner.

I heard Zaia crying, which was typical three-year-old behavior. But then I heard her yell at the nanny, Korinne, which I was not okay with. I wrapped myself in a towel and raced downstairs to restore order. She was having a toddler meltdown and needed to apologize to Korinne. I needed Stephen to intervene because I was literally dripping self-tanner. I stuck my head in the office, where I had assumed he had been holed up.

He wasn't there.

Korinne and I poked our heads outside to confirm that his car was still parked. How could it be there but he was nowhere to be found? It made no sense.

I called him but got no response. I sent a text message—"Babe, where are you?"—and still he did not reply. It was strange that he wasn't answering his phone; he could usually be relied upon to keep me posted on his whereabouts. He was conscientious about checking in throughout the day.

I didn't know what to think. I called our assistant to make sure I hadn't overlooked something. Maybe he had a meeting that I didn't know about? She told me there was nothing on his calendar.

I retrieved Weslie from school, and she walked to Maddox's school to pick him up while Korinne and I began preparing dinner. As soon as Maddox walked through the door, he wanted to know where Daddy was because he was eager for us to get busy hanging ornaments.

The needle on my internal anxiety meter was climbing steadily. I told Korinne that maybe Stephen had gone Christmas shopping and lost track of time. On the surface, I did my best to appear cool. I continued preparing dinner for the kids and asked Korinne to stay late.

When he still wasn't home as I was tucking the littles into bed, I suspected something was seriously wrong. Stephen never blew off the kids. I kept calling him, calling him, calling him, praying he'd pick up.

I phoned his brother. I said I didn't want to freak him out because I was sure there was an explanation, but Stephen was not answering my calls or texts and he wasn't home. His brother suggested that maybe

Stephen's phone battery had died, or maybe he had run into a friend and they'd ended up getting something to eat and lost track of time. I wanted to believe him, but something was not sitting well with me. Stephen's behavior the previous night had been one thing, but for him to totally disappear was next-level bizarre.

I called Robert, Stephen's best friend, to see if he'd heard from him. He agreed Stephen would never fail to respond to me. If Stephen had gotten caught up doing something somewhere, he would still acknowledge my calls. If his phone battery had died, he'd borrow someone else's to call to ask after the kids. For him to go silent was seriously worrisome.

Every fiber of my being wanted to reach out to the police. But I knew from several conversations with Stephen over the years that he would have been disappointed in me if I had done so. He used to say, "I'm a Black man, and if you call the cops they're going to be looking for a Black man." As I heard him saying this a slideshow of images played in my head: mug shots of the likes of Michael Brown, Eric Garner, George Floyd, and Jayland Walker—all Black men killed by cops.

Needing to do *something*, I started reaching out to local hospitals. Maybe he had been in an accident—not in his car, obviously, but somebody else's. I had almost convinced myself that Stephen had decided to jog to the gym from our house, as we occasionally did, and had been struck by a car crossing Ventura Boulevard. We didn't share an Uber account, so I couldn't track his activity there. After confirming that nobody matching Stephen's description had been brought to any of the local emergency rooms, I really started to panic.

Maybe he had been racially profiled and had gotten arrested. It happens all the time. I called the jail to see if anyone fitting his description had been arrested. While I had an officer on the line, I asked about reporting a missing person. I was told that an adult has to be missing for at least twenty-four hours before a report can be filed.

"Could he be at a bar? Or . . . somewhere else?" the officer asked. The implication was clear: This is not an uncommon occurrence and usually the husband is not really missing, merely out drinking or carousing.

I did my best to keep the indignation out of my voice when I replied, "I know my husband, and he's not like that."

As it neared midnight, I was out of my mind with worry. I knew I couldn't wait twenty-four hours to find my husband. I grabbed my keys, left the kids with Korinne, who had offered to spend the night, drove to the Van Nuys police department, and began pounding on the door. They wouldn't let me in because it was after hours. Deflated, I returned home and called the department again only to have whoever answered reiterate the twenty-four-hour rule.

I couldn't access the location of Stephen's phone because we didn't track each other. We weren't that kind of couple, and we were usually together anyway. I couldn't check to see if Stephen had withdrawn money from the bank because we maintained separate accounts.

December 13, 2022, dawned a chilly forty-four degrees in greater Los Angeles, the lowest temperature that would be recorded in the area all month. But the rawness I felt had nothing to do with the weather. I got the kids off to school and then scoured the house. What was I looking for? I had no idea, but I figured I'd know it if I saw it.

There was one thing of note in Stephen's nightstand: a letter dated two weeks earlier in which he made a commitment to wean himself off weed. Stephen had printed his words, originally written in the notes app on his phone, and signed his name to them.

As soon as I was able, I filed a formal missing person report. I implored the officer on duty to help me find my husband. "He has to be hurt somewhere," I said. That was the most likely scenario to me.

The police had other theories. They asked if we had had a fight. If there was abuse in the home. If he had a history of adultery. Every question was like a body blow. My trust in the cops began to waver. I kept thinking about what Stephen had said about Black men and law enforcement. It hit me: *I'm not just missing my husband. I'm missing a Black man. Will they put as much effort into finding him?*

I was convinced that he had to be hurt or lost somewhere. I tried to convey to the police what they didn't understand: "Stephen's the most loyal, loving husband and father." We had just returned from a lovely anniversary weekend, for God's sake. "We're *happy*," I told them—as a little voice in my head whispered, *Right?*

Two officers followed me home to look around. They accessed our security camera footage, which showed Stephen slipping into an Uber car around the time he was supposed to meet me at the gym. He had that omnipresent black backpack slung over his shoulder.

The officers asked me if Stephen owned any guns. I was aware that he had bought one in 2020 during the pandemic. He was scared because the city was experiencing a severe spike in riots and robberies. Several houses in our neighborhood had already been hit. But I had no idea where he kept the gun or if he even knew how to operate it. I vaguely recalled that he might have made one trip to the shooting range. Rooting around, the cops found an unlocked gun case, the gun missing. The likely ramifications of its absence went completely over my head. I had no explanation for why the gun was gone. The cops kept any suspicions to themselves.

In the meantime, Stephen's brother had been able to determine that the last withdrawal in Stephen's account was for under ten dollars, for the Uber ride. Using that information, the officers determined the area that the fare would have covered. At a friend's suggestion, I started calling recovery centers within the radius created by the police. Given his struggles with smoking and drinking, I thought it was plausible that he might have checked himself into rehab. To my surprise, there were a handful of centers near our home.

At the first few I contacted, I was told, "He's an adult. So even if he's in here, we aren't at liberty to tell you without his permission." *Okay, okay, okay.*

The last recovery center I called was six minutes from our home. The woman who answered delivered the same spiel as the others. I pleaded with her. I said I understood privacy laws, and I promised not to report her if he was there and she told me. I just needed to know if he was safe. She calmly replied, "Well, I'm not allowed to tell you if he is here, but if he was, would you want to leave him a message?"

My heart nearly exploded in my chest. I took her words as a non-confirmation confirmation. "Yes!" I said. "Please tell him I love him so much. And I'm so proud of him for making this choice. Our family will stand behind him through anything, and he can stay there as long as he needs. If he doesn't want to talk to me, it's okay. I'll never judge him, and I'll be here for him whenever he's ready to resume contact."

I began calling friends and family to say I had found Stephen, that he was safe. I ran outside to the front yard to catch the cops, who were standing near their parked squad car. I said, "Hey, I think I found him, but they can't legally confirm with me. Can you please go ask from your side?" I returned to the house, awash in relief.

The letter in his nightstand, his panic the night before—it all made sense now. Stephen had gone to rehab. He was going through something and now he was getting help. I was so caught up in my thoughts, I barely registered the *whomp, whomp, whomp* of helicopters flying overhead and the wail of police sirens. Something was happening near our house, but then again, we live in Los Angeles, the land of high-speed car chases. Something always seems to be happening.

About twenty minutes later, the two cops out in front were joined by a third officer. He was older, very sweet. He came to the door, trailed by the others. The new arrival looked at me with such compassion in his eyes. He asked me to sit down, and my heart sank. They don't ask you to sit unless what they're about to tell you is very, very bad.

I couldn't bring myself to sit down. If I didn't sit, then maybe whatever he was about to tell me wouldn't be real.

A dark energy settled over the room as I stood frozen in place. "Your husband has been found," he said. "He's not in rehab." He sat down at the kitchen table. I stayed where I was. "Your husband was found in a hotel. He was found by the maid. He shot himself."

No. No. No. No.

I told them they had found a Black man, but it didn't mean they had found *my* man. Stephen would never do what this officer was suggesting.

Ever-so-gently, the officer explained Stephen had left a letter and his

ID. He had been identified by his tattoos, including that one below his elbow: *I am . . . I have . . . I deserve . . .*

My stomach clenched. He had spent eight painful hours getting inked during a magical trip we took to New Zealand. It was like a DNA strand with tribal markings meant to honor the country's indigenous Maori people, and the loves of his life: me and Weslie and music. It was his version of a charm bracelet, and he had always intended to add on to it. He spoke often of a return trip to New Zealand and a visit to the same artist to mark Maddox and Zaia's presence on the strand. A trip that would now never happen. His beautiful tattoo reduced to a macabre identifying mark.

I raced down the hallway, shrieking. The sound that escaped from my throat was feral. I'd never heard the likes of it before. I collapsed onto the floor in a fetal position, where I would stay for several minutes, keening as one of our assistants held me tight.

Nothing made any sense. I was so scared. I felt so alone even as I was in another's embrace. The world went black. The walls closed in on me until I thought I was going to suffocate. Until that moment, I had never understood the phrase "It's like the world stopped." That's exactly how it felt: as if time froze. I literally couldn't believe that Stephen was dead.

When you experience a tragedy of this magnitude, you can't explain fully in words the pain and shock that you feel. My spine, it seemed, would not hold me upright. I felt like an inflatable tube person in a wind tunnel. Later I'd come across something that helped me understand what my body was experiencing. In Chinese medicine, the lungs are associated with grief and the spleen with worry, so it's no wonder that my back could not support me.

I screamed until I was out of breath. After composing myself somewhat, I repeated to the police that this must all be a terrible misunderstanding. "It's not him!" I said. "I found him in rehab. He wouldn't do what you're saying he did. Stephen despises guns!"

The irony was almost too much for me to bear. He had killed himself with a gun he bought to protect us.

Over the next few hours, one mystery would be solved. The reason I hadn't been able to reach Stephen is he had switched his phone to airplane mode so he couldn't be contacted or tracked. That was the only answer I'd have for a while.

I didn't ask the cops for any more details about how he died. I didn't want to know. I found out much later that he had folded his clothing neatly in a pile in the hotel room before killing himself, which was confusing beyond all reason. When had Stephen ever been neat, and why start when he was on the verge of a final, messy act?

What Stephen did was outrageous. He was the most nonviolent person I've ever known. The man who was a friend to all must have felt so utterly alone to decide that this was his only or best option. And it wasn't an impulsive act. He had planned it, which would be impossible to overlook when I stumbled across the key to his gun case while doing my makeup one morning. He had set it on my vanity for me to find because the case is where he kept his personal passwords and other codes.

It's really hard to be told your husband is dead. But to be told your husband *chose* to be dead—that's impossible to fathom. The first few days afterward I was in a daze. It took me a while to process that he was really gone. I still expected a call from Stephen, telling me that he had had a freak accident but was okay. I couldn't accept that he was not coming back.

Stephen and I had a habit of sending each other photographs we snapped of elderly people we came across who were clearly couples. No caption was needed. *This is going to be us someday*, we understood the photos to mean. The reality that Stephen and I would not grow old together, that we would not be, as we always kidded, "the coolest grandparents ever," was beyond my comprehension.

My thoughts grew darker. Stephen had always described our home as our safe place. It was where he could recharge by plugging into his family's abundant love and laughter. He often expressed feeling the most himself around me, Weslie, Maddox, and Zaia. If only tWitch would have let his mask fall once in a while in public. If only Stephen had opened up to us about how much he was hurting. We would have listened, sympathized, and supported him. We wouldn't have judged.

Obviously, he feared the vulnerability that came with seeking help. He wanted to be everyone's superhero, not someone who needed protecting himself. I believe he was terrified that acknowledging his need for an emotional break or therapeutic intervention would shatter the illusion of his public persona and disappoint those who cared about him. If that's accurate, he could not have gotten it more wrong.

I couldn't get it out of my head that he'd spent his final hours alone less than a mile away in a nondescript 1960s-era roadside motel, the Oak Tree Inn, where the rooms open up directly to parking spaces. What had propelled him there?

A memory surfaced. In 2020, Stephen's beloved thirteen-year-old Jack Russell terrier mix, Krypto, deteriorated rapidly before our eyes. In a matter of weeks, he went from an ambulatory old boy to a wobbly invalid that ran into walls and had to be scooped out of the pool after falling in.

Krypto never left our front yard, so we hadn't seen the need to put up a fence or tie him up on a leash. But around this time, I was watching Stephen and Maddox shoot baskets in our driveway when I realized Krypto had disappeared. For the first time ever, he had wandered off. Stephen sprinted down the street and came back holding the dog in his arms. The vet later explained to us that when a sick dog is on the verge of dying, it will separate itself from its pack so as not to be a burden. We were Stephen's pack, and I really do believe he disappeared down the road, separating himself from us, because he was very, very, very sick and didn't want to weigh us down.

Yet how could Stephen do this when we had big plans for our careers, were committed to having more children, had employees and corporate partners who believed in us and depended on us? The people closest to us knew we had very much been looking to the future. So openly had Stephen spoken about wanting to have more children that several people would pull me aside in the days ahead to ask if I was pregnant.

Stephen also had talked endlessly about adopting three rottweiler puppies, and he was very particular about what he was looking for. He was researching the breed and emailing Weslie and me about his findings. I told him that if we were going to add three big dogs and another kid to the family, we needed a bigger backyard, so we had also been sending each other local listings of houses for sale that had ample outdoor space.

But I couldn't mourn the Boss babies who would never be. I had to be fully present for Weslie, Maddox, and Zaia because their world had just been torn asunder.

CHAPTER 11

WHAT DO WE DO NOW?

I had my assistant collect Weslie from school. As soon as my fourteen-year-old baby girl walked in the door, I grabbed her hands, guided her to the couch, and sat down next to her. I was weeping, which alarmed her. Weslie had never seen me cry before, except when we watched Disney movies together. She had been Stephen's "ace," and I knew she was going to be absolutely devastated.

Just a few weeks earlier, he had been very protective toward her when she attended her first homecoming dance. He had joked with her that if she got out on the floor with a boy, he would whip out a ruler and measure the distance between them and admonish him: "Hold on, player. You're a little close." Seeing her so grown-up had turned him contemplative about the future. They had recently had a conversation about which song they should play during their father-daughter dance at her wedding—a dance that now would never happen.

"I'm sorry, Weslie," I said, choking on my tears. "Stephen unalived himself."

Unalived—it rhymes with *five*, a number that no longer fit our family. It was a weird choice of words, but I found that my speech reflected the awkwardness of Stephen's death and my reluctance to accept it. "After what happened to us . . ." I'd say. "After the situation happened with Stephen . . ." Or "After everything that unfolded . . ." The indirectness of my speech stood in sharp contrast to the unambiguity of his death.

Through heaving sobs, Weslie wailed, "Mommy, no! No, Mommy! No, Mommy—no!" while I held her tight. Over and over, she screamed. Her cries will echo in my head for the rest of my life.

"Why? Why? Why? Why? Why did he do this?" she asked. "This isn't real!" she added as she ran out to the backyard.

I caught up to her and we clung to each other. I let her purge her feelings as we sat for a long time out by the firepit, wrapped in a blanket and clinging to each other. The police and the crisis counselors, bless them, stayed at the house for a while. They were there in case we needed to talk but kept a respectful distance so we could cry in privacy. We couldn't see them—they sat at the kitchen table—but we could sense their support.

Maddox and Zaia would be home soon, but I wasn't ready to break the news to them. I waited a couple of days, unsure how to convey to a six-year-old that his father, his hero, was gone forever. That he would never help Maddox decorate another family Christmas tree or play another video game with him. That first day my ebullient, boisterous boy was strangely subdued, content to sit with Zaia and play with toys. He conspicuously did not ask where Daddy was, as if intuiting on some level that it was a question better left unsaid.

The next morning, I was seated on the couch in our living room after a sleepless night when Maddox came padding down the stairs.

"Mommy, where is Daddy?" he said.

While I was gathering my thoughts, he asked again, a little more insistently, "Where's Daddy?"

I took his hand and said, "Baby, come with me." I steered him back toward the stairs because Weslie had told me she wanted to be present when I broke the news to him. "Come to Weslie's room, baby," I said. "Everything's going to be okay."

We arrived at Weslie's room, stepped inside, and shut the door. He asked again, "Where is Daddy?"

I took a big breath and said, "Daddy's in the sky above us, looking down and protecting us."

Maddox said, "But I want him to be here. I want him to be here with us now."

I explained that he will always be here. He will always be with us everywhere.

Maddox didn't quite understand. "But why can't he be here?" he said. "I want him to be here."

I pointed to Maddox's heart and asked him what it was.

"It's my heart," he said, and at that moment he seemed to grasp what I was telling him. His face collapsed. He understood that he was never going to see his daddy again. "My heart!" he shouted.

The only thing I knew to do right then was give him a big hug. Weslie and I hugged him as hard as we could. The three of us continued to hold on to one another tightly as our tears flowed.

After a while, Maddox abruptly stopped sobbing. We all did. It was like our emotions had hit a wall.

Maddox became quiet and eerily still. He stayed like that for a few minutes. Finally he looked up at me and said, "Okay." And that was it.

He was so brave. It broke me that he had to be that brave.

"What do you want to do now?" I asked him.

And in the most Maddox fashion ever, he said, "I want to eat."

I grabbed his hand, and we all made our way downstairs. As we were walking, I kept saying, "Stay with me. Stay with me."

"Okay," he replied.

We walked into the living room, which was filled with extended family. I kept whispering, "Stay with me," and he kept saying, "Okay."

I reheated some leftover pizza, and we sat on the couch. It wasn't long, maybe a few minutes, before Maddox was laughing and acting silly.

I thought to myself, *I have the brightest, bravest boy in the world. How lucky am I?*

And how unlucky is Maddox to have to grow up without his father?

The indelible bruise that he and his siblings will carry in their hearts is hard to bear. It is gut-wrenching that despite his best intentions, Stephen passed on his generational trauma to his only son.

The day after Maddox found out the news about Stephen, he came downstairs dressed in shorts. No matter how cold it gets, I cannot coax him into putting on pants. "Please don't make me," he'll plead. I would never. If Maddox wants to get revenge on his dead dad by wearing shorts every day for the rest of his life, who am I to stand in his way?

Zaia was the last to learn the truth, though how much could we convey to a three-year-old that she would understand?

Like Maddox, she knew something was wrong. "Where's Daddy?" she asked, reclining on the bench at the foot of my bed.

Cradling her tiny face, I gently explained, "Daddy is in the sky watching over us. He's an angel now."

In her innocent voice, she responded, "Oh, I want to be an angel too."

Her words took my breath away. I managed to croak, "Yes, one day you'll be an angel, but not for a very, very, *very* long time."

From that point on, I took the kids outside nightly to gaze at the stars. We spoke about their dad residing in the sky among those stars, and sometimes the younger ones would point at one and say, "There's Daddy." After tucking the kids into bed, I would return to the backyard by myself. Whether I soaked in the hot tub or floated in the pool, I'd let my tears mix with the water and I'd scream at those distant stars.

When it comes to discussing challenging topics with children, I've learned that the most important considerations are their age and how they process information. Tailoring the conversation so that each child feels seen and understood is a great foundation for creating an environment where they feel free to express themselves unselfconsciously. There is no one-size-fits-all script or a flawless way to address difficult topics. All we can do is initiate the conversation, acknowledge the children's perspectives, and foster an atmosphere where they feel comfortable sharing their thoughts and feelings.

In those first few days without Stephen, I didn't eat, sleep, or even drink water. I couldn't function in any capacity. I was simply floating through the days in a daze. Flowers and food arrived by the truckload. I must have had five thousand unread messages on my phone, but I couldn't bring myself to open them. I was at my absolute limit. I did not know what to do or how to be.

No one knew what to say or do around me. There was nothing anyone could say or do. These were such dark days. I was still trying to take care of everyone around me, and as it sank in that I was going to have to try to take care of everyone around me forever—and do it all by myself, without Stephen's help—well, it was just an unspeakably sad realization.

I was in such a state of shock that my mind played tricks on me. Multiple times I had the actual thought that Stephen wasn't the one who was gone; I must have been in a car crash that had left me in a coma, and it was in this altered state that my husband and best friend was dead. Any second I was going to wake up, and the first face I would see would be Stephen's. I would slap myself to make sure that I was not sleeping.

By the afternoon of the third day, December 15, I was alarmingly weak and unsteady on my feet. I heard Zaia screaming when she was supposed to be napping, and there was an edge to her cries that I hadn't heard before. I instinctively recognized that edge for what it was: a toddler's way of expressing anxiety. She was picking up on the sad energy in the house, and it was making her panicky. I slipped into her room and lay down beside her. For the next thirty minutes I rocked her back and forth, back and forth, as she hung on to me for dear life. I whispered to her to close her eyes and go to sleep, that everything was going to be okay. That we were safe. I closed my eyes, too, because I couldn't tell my child to get some rest and not show her how it's done.

For the first time since my anniversary weekend with Stephen, I fell into a dream state. I experienced a slideshow of memories; then everything went black. I started shaking, and the whole room became a moving set. A face appeared like the full moon in the night sky. It kept morphing into three faces, only one of which I recognized. It was Stephen.

His lips started to move. I could clearly make out what he was saying: *I'm sorry. I love you.*

His face started to fade. I followed it as it disappeared down a tunnel. There was total blackness, which gave way to a blinding whiteness that brought me back to a waking state. I sat up feeling refreshed. I guess I needed that appearance, however fleeting, from Stephen to feel reassured. At peace. My husband no longer existed, but for the first time since he died, I could feel his presence.

"Thank you, my love," I said, "for comforting me."

Our house was quickly surrounded by paparazzi. I did not want my vulnerability or the children's sorrow to become a commodity, our grief captured in photographs for the world to gawk at. I absolutely refused to allow my children or myself to become fodder for the tabloids. I was determined not to provide anybody with the money photo they sought of me, my face swollen from crying, clad in sweats that hung from my shrunken frame, flanked by my sad children. No way was I going to give anybody a photo that could haunt my kids on the internet for the rest of their lives. The solution, as I saw it, was simply to refuse to leave the house. I hunkered down with my children, which created a quandary given that I now had a funeral to organize.

We were all lost, but none more so than Maddox, who struggled to figure out his place in our new family paradigm. Being the only guy in the house is complex for him. He's a joyful spirit who wears his heart on his sleeve. If I slipped into Weslie's room to avoid the memories that the bed I shared with Stephen held, Maddox would follow me and say, "Can I sleep in Weslie's room too?" He was ever vigilant, the child who needed protecting acting like he had to be the man of the house, his child brain stuck in a spinning rainbow-colored wheel as we rebooted.

People tell me not to worry, because kids are resilient. But I hate that they have to be so resilient. Because Stephen's death came from so far out of left field, my children learned far too young about the unpredictability of life. I was flying blind when it came to steering them through this trauma, but I knew this much: We had to talk about what happened, because if we didn't the kids would construct their own versions of the truth, and those might be even more devastating. I do not want Maddox going through life believing, as he said to me in an achingly small voice not long after Stephen died, "Maybe if I had been nicer, Daddy would still be here."

I want to make sure my children feel seen and heard even in their lowest moments. I don't want them ever to feel weird or self-conscious for asking anything or for not knowing something. I want them to know I'm not perfect and I don't have all the answers, but together we can figure things out. I had always been uncomfortable asking my mom questions when I was growing up because she'd invariably say "Oh, we don't talk about that" or "You're just a kid. You wouldn't understand." *Really?* I wanted to say, *Try me.* She may have been trying to protect me, but her dismissiveness left me feeling as if my thoughts and feelings weren't important.

Those first few weeks after Stephen's death were so hard. The confusion and sadness were too much to confront, so I distracted myself with ever-growing to-do lists. When in overdrive like that, I didn't have to think or feel. I just kept moving.

My friends are forever giving me grief because the batteries on my laptop and phone can be counted on to die from a lack of charge at least a couple of times a day—often in the middle of a meeting or call—rendering me temporarily incommunicado. I've been known to drain my own battery in a similar fashion, going and going and going until I have absolutely nothing left physically or emotionally. That tendency grew more pronounced after Stephen's death. I rationalized my almost manic busyness by telling myself that my children had just lost one parent; I had no choice but to show up for them. They are my tether to the world. The responsibility rests with me to show my children that there's so much purpose and light and love in this world for them to still embrace.

What Stephen had done was not a reflection on us. It was our choice how to respond to what had happened.

CHAPTER 12

PAYING OUR RESPECTS

There was never any question that we would memorialize Stephen. He had a positive impact on so many people. I wasn't going to let any discomfort about how he died preclude us from celebrating his beautiful, joyful life. I wanted the service to be dignified and intimate and private so the mourners—the people whom Stephen had deeply loved and been loved by—would feel safe to be vulnerable. In other words, I wanted no paparazzi or press anywhere near the service.

In the days after his death, my mother, father, siblings, and members of Stephen's extended family gathered at the house. So did the team that Stephen and I had assembled to help us manage our businesses. Everyone was grieving. What I was about to discover is that this kind of inconsolable, inexplicable loss hits everybody differently. It can cause otherwise lovely people to become weirdly competitive about who is suffering the most profoundly. It was perplexing to watch some individuals assert the depth of their connection to Stephen and vice versa, as if they were contestants in a TV reality show angling for the most sympathy.

A few of the people closest to Stephen couldn't accept—and still haven't accepted—his death. They are so angry at him. Because he was such a wonderful person, to harbor any dark thoughts about him seems like a referendum on *their* character. Of course they want to express their rage over what he did, but it feels mean, like piling on, and so they go out of their way to accentuate his goodness. It was deeply disconcerting when someone on Stephen's side of the family told a British tabloid in the days after his death that they were "not sure" Stephen had died by suicide, casting public doubt on the Los Angeles County medical examiner's conclusion and drawing more attention to the way Stephen died than how he lived.

I had only been to one funeral in my life—my paternal grandmother's in Minnesota—and I had certainly never given a second's thought to planning one. You have to process so much all at once: your own grief, others' grief, differing opinions on how the dead ought to be honored. I didn't even know what a wake was until I had to plan Stephen's. The myriad details were overwhelming. I have so much sympathy for anyone having to plan a funeral now that I know what's involved. It's the toughest task I've ever had to undertake.

Because of the scheduling difficulties during the holidays, we settled on the first week in January for the service. Stephen's family presented me with a list of roughly five dozen people from his side who would be attending. Most of them were from out of state. I had offered to pay everyone's expenses, which wasn't a problem, but a conflict arose over the matter of the wake and how Stephen's body would be displayed. Did I want an open or closed casket?

I could only imagine the trauma his body had absorbed. I could only imagine it because I had purposely avoided any details of where or how he shot himself. I didn't want to have that image in my head. An assistant had stepped in and saved me from having to provide a positive identification. I was pretty sure that however he looked wasn't how he'd want to be remembered. My stance was reinforced when the funeral director inadvertently let slip that Stephen had shot himself in the head. Ugh. There's an image I'll never unsee. I made a call to my pastor, who reassured me that a closed casket was the obvious call.

However, Stephen's family insisted on an open casket, citing African

American tradition. I tried to reason with Stephen's mother. Funerals are to honor the dead, not mollify the living. Did she really believe that Stephen would want his loved ones' last image of him to reflect the trauma of the most shameful act of his life? I reasoned that Stephen wouldn't have wanted her or anybody else to see him like that, and anybody who didn't know that didn't know Stephen. She was unmoved.

I understood the subtext. She was mad at me because she couldn't be angry at Stephen. Nothing I did or didn't do was going to make her feel better. I wanted to give her grace, so I offered a compromise: I said it would be okay if a small group of seven to ten people—including his mother, grandparents, brothers, uncle, and aunt—wanted to view the open casket before it was closed for the rest of the wake.

The next list we received from his family for the open-casket portion contained a few dozen names and included people I had never seen at the many family reunions I had attended with Stephen. A few people on the list hadn't seen Stephen since he was a toddler, if ever. I stood firm—no more than thirteen people, tops. Also, I said—and I thought this was obvious—no photographs or video could be taken during the open-casket viewing. I couldn't risk any photo getting leaked to the press or splashed across social media platforms and becoming the lasting image that people would have of him.

My children absolutely, positively could not stumble upon such a photograph at some later date. That's not how I wanted anybody, much less his kids, to remember Stephen. It was bad enough that strangers online were creating YouTube videos and such to "investigate" Stephen's death. The idea that there was some conspiracy was downright mean-spirited. It breaks my heart to think that my kids might one day stumble upon these theories. Isn't it bad enough that they'll have to live with what Stephen did? Do they have to be potentially exposed to such cruelty too?

At the advice of my lawyers, I insisted that everybody who viewed the open casket sign a nondisclosure agreement to protect Stephen's privacy, a requirement that exasperated his family. "If we have to sign NDAs," they said, "then everybody has to sign NDAs."

"No problem," I replied.

My team sent out last-minute emails to all the invited guests alerting them that they'd have to sign an NDA.

I chose not to view the open casket. The wake was held on the second floor of the funeral home. I arrived early for the closed-casket viewing and stayed downstairs to greet guests. One of Stephen's relatives, before proceeding upstairs, got in the face of my assistant Adrienne, who was checking people in. He was indignant about his teenage daughter being excluded from the open-casket viewing, and he was loudly voicing his discontent to Adrienne. He was also refusing to sign the NDA. My dad stepped in to calm the relative down, to no avail. He continued to wag his finger at Adrienne and at me.

I lost it. I ran out of the funeral home sobbing. Stephen's best friend was approaching the building as I was leaving it, and he consoled me. I explained what was happening and he went inside to talk to Stephen's relative, who could not be placated, though he did sign the NDA and make his way upstairs.

The service was the next day, and everybody had managed to keep the details under wraps—until that morning, when someone on my business team fielded a call from TMZ. The time and location had been leaked to the website. So at the last minute we had to come up with defensive and avoidance maneuvers and other diversionary tactics to ensure that the kids and I were not followed or photographed on the drive to Forest Lawn Memorial-Parks in Glendale. Even so, one of my brothers was nearly run off the road by a paparazzo.

The funeral was intimate, as befitted the introverted Stephen. I had already decided that I would hold another memorial in February so his friends in the dance community and others whose lives he touched could pay their final tributes to tWitch in a less formal, less somber service. Roughly three hundred people attended the Celebration of Life, as we called it. It was held in Hollywood, at the Mosaic church that Stephen and I had regularly attended.

My connection to Mosaic predated my relationship with Stephen.

The fellowship I found there was my lifeline when I was just putting down roots in Los Angeles. The community embraced me unconditionally, which I needed lest I lose myself in the competitiveness that underscores so many day-to-day conversations, turning the simple question, "What are you doing now?" into one potentially loaded with assessment or judgment.

With its all-white interior and expansive windows at the base of the hills, the venue enveloped us in a warmth that is one of the reasons we liked the church so much. Those closest to him took turns delivering heartfelt speeches, sharing memories and moments with Stephen, recounting the beautiful life he lived, and acknowledging the people he inspired. Each speech carried a unique perspective, capturing diverse experiences and aspects of his wonderful character.

I nervously took the lead in opening the memorial, confronted by the collective sadness and pain still reflected on the faces of our loved ones. I spoke from the heart and allowed the energy from the crowd to guide me. I talked about how inspiring Stephen was, the love we shared, and how confusing it was that he was dead because he had been such a gung ho celebrant of life.

Weslie followed me and delivered a beautiful and moving speech. One thing she said about Stephen was so true everybody in the building nodded in agreement: He gave the best hugs. Speaking from the heart, Weslie shared some of her favorite memories of times spent with Stephen but also said that she was really upset with him for what he did. It was heartbreaking to see someone I love so much bear so much weight and strength for so many people, but her poise and bravery left me profoundly proud to be her mother.

She told everyone the last thing Stephen said to her, about wanting to be her Superman. Some people might have chuckled because that was such a Stephen thing to say, but I hope they also recognized that Weslie will have to carry the weight of that sentence with her forever. I believe he said what he did to her because he wanted to be honest. That's the kind of relationship they had. But let's face it, what he said cuts deep. I hope she's not destined to go through life wondering if she might have said or done anything to alter the chain of events.

Ellen DeGeneres, too, spoke with raw honesty, voicing out loud the anger that many in the building were feeling. She was the first person I heard say out loud how mad she was at Stephen for leaving us the way he did. By giving voice to her rage, she made it comfortable for everyone, including me, to express our rage at his final act. The talented actress and comedienne Loni Love injected humor in her speech, providing much-needed laughter. Actor, singer, and TV host Wayne Brady shared eloquent and moving words; Stephen's closest friends delivered reminiscences that were incredibly touching; and Slavik and Aubrey Fisher performed a dance that made the walls of the church pulse with passion.

The event featured a captivating video compilation showcasing moments with our family, his dancing, and interactions with friends, as well as snippets from the various shows he worked on. The celebration focused on Stephen's considerable investment in the dance industry as well as the lasting imprint he left on others.

In the months that followed, I was made aware that members of his family were criticizing me on social media for my handling of the funeral, for the NDAs, and for failing to attend a Boss family reunion that I hadn't even been invited to. For his mother, whose husband had died by suicide when Stephen was in his teens, the pain had to be off the charts. I did my best to meet her where she was and to practice empathy for a woman who had given birth to the love of my life.

But then, one of them told me in a phone call that I was responsible for Stephen's death—it was my fault. The person would later apologize, and I would forgive them. But there could be no forgetting those words. To lose someone to suicide is the most brutal, painful experience, one I wouldn't wish on anyone. To tell anyone that someone's suicide is their fault is the most selfish, spiteful act I can imagine. As I remind my kids every day, your words matter. Like toothpaste squeezed from the tube, words can't be put back in the speaker's mouth.

In the months after Stephen's death, a narrative spread like a virus on social media that I'd denied Stephen's mom access to the kids. Nobody on Stephen's side of the family set the record straight by noting that I flew her from Arizona to California and back so she could attend a Grandparents' Day school function, arranged for the kids to regularly FaceTime with her, and regularly sent her photos.

Aside from the funeral and another private service we held at the Mosaic church, the kids and I spent two months holed up in the house playing board games and cards and doing arts and crafts and feeling all our feelings. I conducted all my business meetings remotely. And people, if they wanted to hang out with us, braved the paparazzi to come to the house.

One of our first visitors was a dancer friend, Courtney Galiano, who expressed concern over my mental health. Her mother-in-law had con- nections to a mental health nonprofit that offered in-house therapists. With my blessing, Courtney made the phone call right then and there, and I spoke briefly to someone who put me instantly at ease. I started telehealth sessions, and the therapist would also end up working with Weslie. I found a licensed children's therapist for Maddox and Zaia. Before Stephen's suicide, I had been to a therapist once. The person was a bad fit for me, and I never went back. Finding someone with whom I clicked made all the difference. Having someone outside my inner circle to talk to turned out to be a game changer, especially in navigating through grief and trauma on such a public stage.

The benefits went beyond having someone to whom I could expel some of my most toxic thoughts. It was so helpful to get practical advice on how to handle the chaos. Therapy became the anchor I didn't know I needed, the ballast in a storm I never saw coming.

Addressing pain isn't easy. I normally love to talk, but talk therapy can be hard work. It can be a royal pain getting up earlier than you want to and driving yourself to a session or sitting through a very uncomfortable conversation. But it's not a luxury; it's essential.

I kept Weslie out of high school, Maddox out of first grade, and Zaia out of preschool and scheduled therapy sessions for all of us over Zoom.

We stuck together like castaways on a raft, clinging to one another as we rode out our roiling emotions: anger, betrayal, bewilderment, devastation, guilt, and sadness. We experienced some awfully low lows during this time, but I can thankfully say I never got down enough to comprehend in any way, shape, or form why Stephen had concluded that tomorrow wasn't a gift worth unwrapping. We felt gratitude, too, because God had put us in a space where we were together and safe and protected by a support system of nonjudgmental family members who flew in on the first flights they could catch from Utah, and friends who fed and hugged us. Cried with us. Listened to us. Ran errands for us. Knowing we were trapped inside, a girlfriend sent a box full of crafts for the kids to do at home. The gestures were a reminder that the simple act of doing something small for someone in a crisis can be a lifeline, a testament to the power of care and compassion.

For a couple of weeks, my brother Dave whipped up breakfast for me and the kids (and anyone else who stopped by the house). No questions asked, no inquiries about hunger or preferences; he just did it.

My other brother, Aaron, erected a playground in our backyard. He didn't know what to say, but he recognized that the kids were going to need some kind of recreation because they were housebound. He literally built them a swing set from scratch in two days. I didn't even know where the tools were, but he found them and built this amazing structure even though he had never done anything like it before. My sister Becky shadowed me discreetly just in case I needed her for anything.

And my mom did a thorough cleaning, ridding the house of reminders of a happy occasion now postponed indefinitely. I had boxes everywhere, but mostly in the garage, because I had planned something called "the Boss Games" for later in the month. It was our version of the *America Ninja Warrior* TV show, and it was going to be a big deal. Each of my siblings and their kids would form a team; each team would have its own T-shirts, colors, and nicknames; and we would compete in a full slate of activities. We had planned to rent a big house where everyone would stay. I had ordered all the shirts, cones, pieces of equipment for the games, and prizes. Everything was in boxes that I hadn't had time to open. My mom went through them and sent back what could be sent back and stored what little was worth keeping.

Thank goodness she left untouched other boxes that I would stumble upon later, because the contents caused me to question just about everything about Stephen that I thought I knew to be true. The secrets they contained I've hidden from my mother and everyone else. Until now.

CHAPTER 13

A STAGGERING DISCOVERY

When combing through Stephen's journals after his death, I gained a sickening clarity, if not a concrete sense of why he did what he did.

A few of his entries would allude to sexual abuse he endured as a child at the hands of an adult male—a trauma he detailed in strict confidence to his friend, who relayed the conversation to me only after Stephen's death. I don't expect I'll ever have a definitive answer, but from what he wrote on the page, I couldn't help but wonder: *Did the abuse happen when he was roughly the same age as Maddox? Did becoming a biological father dislodge those buried memories of his childhood abuse, and did he worry that he was somehow fated to do to his son the same monstrous things that had been done to him?*

What I can't understand is Stephen sat quietly as one of our mutual friends, who had been sexually abused as a youngster by an adult figure whom they unabashedly loved, shared the details of the abuse and the difficulties they had reconciling the ghoul with the guardian. Stephen was sympathetic and supportive, as always, but he never let on that he might be able to relate to the horrors. But it was there in his journal pages, not spelled out explicitly but expressed in so many words and doodles, that

Stephen might have killed himself because he thought he was protecting us from an even more horrifying act he thought he might be capable of.

Stephen's decision to take his life made his death a profoundly difficult and complex situation. I felt abandoned, betrayed by the person I trusted the most, the one person in the world who had my best interests at heart, always. He had my back—yeah, he really did. I know he hurt me, but I also know he loved me. I had trusted him with every ounce of my being, and in the end he betrayed that trust by disappearing on me. He had broken his vows in the most *screw you* way.

The way that Stephen loved us was so big, so his suicide came with a staggering grief tax. The grander the love, the greater the grief. I've come to view bereavement as the nonnegotiable cost of losing someone you cherished. But as I dealt with the detritus of Stephen's life, it began to feel as if the price of having loved him might literally and emotionally bankrupt me.

I retrieved his laptop and his phone and scrolled through his histories. I read his journals. The mere act of snooping felt disloyal, because in all our years together Stephen had never given me a single reason not to trust him. What was I hoping to find? Anything that would have made his suicide make sense. Had there been other women? Men? A rumor was circulating that Stephen was gay, so I looked for evidence of that. Was he being blackmailed? Stalked?

I had always considered us great communicators, but I would discover that there was an awful lot about him that I didn't know. His search history contained weed websites, magic mushroom websites, and inquiries such as *Do my kids love my nanny more than me? How do I become a better father? How do I communicate with my kids?* The questions struck me as so bizarre because I considered him an amazing dad.

Whatever happened to him as a child, he never could get past it. It caused him tremendous shame and guilt. No matter how much success he achieved or how beloved he was, it was as if he were a seven-year-old boy trapped in trauma. Stephen's search history revealed that in summer 2022 he had looked up a suicide hotline. I could find no evidence on his phone that he made the call. I'm sure he felt a lot of shame for even having sought out the number.

A suicide note written on pages torn from a yellow pad was found near his body, addressed to me, our kids, and his family. I was terrified to read the multipage letter. I assumed it would solve the mystery of why he killed himself, and I was apprehensive about knowing his unvarnished truth. I think most people assume a suicide note exists to be the confession before the final unburdening, but in Stephen's case, it left us with more questions than closure. It was beautiful, but he spoke elliptically, and in circles, same as in his journal entries.

Even in his final moments, he couldn't give shape to the demons that had defeated him. He couldn't express what he was going through that had siphoned all his hope. Instead, he expressed so much love. And shame, a word he mentioned multiple times. One sentence stuck out— something about a little boy. He was still the little boy. He couldn't get past the little boy who had been abandoned and shamed.

It was strangely comforting to see his scratchy writing. I could picture him holding the pen in the weird way that he did, not like a chopstick resting between his right index and middle fingers and thumb, but with all four fingers gripping it like he was stirring a thick, boiling liquid in a pot. How many hours had I spent watching him bent over a journal like it was a cauldron, filling page after page with his hilariously dense writing?

The pad from which the pages were ripped contained the start of another letter, suggesting he intended to write each of us individual notes, but he never got further than the salutation. I can only guess that he became overwhelmed trying to express his deep and abiding love for the family he had created. The idea of saying an individual goodbye was too painful, as evidenced by the dried teardrops on the page.

Those teardrops made me think of his state of mind that last night he spent with us. It is especially tough for me to look back on that evening because there are so many things I wish I had done differently. If only I had asked more penetrating questions about where he had gone and the lie he was referring to. There had to have been one thing I could have asked that would have uncorked his bottled-up emotions and released an explanation for his strange behavior.

A team of crisis counselors met with me and the kids at the house, and one of the things I remember them saying is that people who die by suicide often have had at least one failed attempt before they are successful. The hair on the back of my neck stood up when I heard that. Had Stephen left the house the night before he disappeared with the intent of killing himself only to talk himself out of it? Was the lie that he had not been to the dispensary at all? That he didn't expect to be around for the Christmas tree trimming?

Or had he been lying to me as a form of self-sabotage? Ahead of his funeral I made a staggering discovery that would cause me to wonder if he had been hiding some appalling behavior from me to convince himself that he was a terrible person whom we were all better off without.

My stylist and close friend Lisa was helping me pick out Stephen's final outfit. It didn't really matter in the grand scheme of things because he was going to be cremated, but I wanted him to look as nice as possible for his family for the open-casket wake.

Sneakers were an obsession of his. Stephen had over one hundred pairs, including a few, never worn, that still contained their sales tags. I started sifting through the boxes, looking for the perfect pair to carry him into the afterlife. What I found was a lot more than shoes. There were ziplocked bags of psychedelic mushrooms—some of the bags were full; some were half-empty; a few contained only one or two mushrooms. There were other substances that I had to look up on my phone. It was a cornucopia of drugs. I was stunned.

I literally could not believe what I was seeing. The cognitive dissonance I experienced was unlike anything I've ever known. Until that moment, I had zero knowledge that Stephen used any drugs besides marijuana. Rummaging around, I found sickening surprises in almost every other shoebox—mushrooms and cash and tactical knives and pills that I couldn't identify. I even found pills in an emptied-out Altoids tin, which really freaked me out. He'd been hiding his use practically in plain sight, and any of these substances, or the knives, could have been easily accessed by the kids.

I know for a fact that Stephen would never have wanted our kids to stumble onto the drugs. He'd never intentionally put them in danger. But the sheer volume of drugs hidden in a variety of places suggested to me that Stephen had lost track of his stockpile. His mind was so muddled that he couldn't keep his stash straight, just as he may have been struggling to keep his two personas, tWitch and Stephen, straight. When he wrote the note vowing to give up weed, I wonder if he really meant *all* the drugs, but he hadn't been ready to own up to everything that he was ingesting.

It was hard to decide which was more disconcerting: that he was self-medicating to such an extent or that he didn't feel safe enough to confide in me about whatever was causing him such pain. He was so ashamed of his marijuana use; I can't imagine that he wanted me to discover that he was using harder drugs. Either his mental state had seriously deteriorated or I didn't know my husband nearly as well as I thought I did.

While scrolling through his texts, I discovered that not only had Stephen arranged a meeting with a drug dealer while we were in Laguna Beach for our magical anniversary weekend, but he also bought more drugs that he picked up after we got home. He might have even done so that Sunday night when he texted me all freaked out. I replayed that weird conversation we had. It did not escape my notice that the hotel he would check into the next day had a tree theme. Was the tree emoji meant to tell me that he had ended up there intending to commit self-harm?

Was he in the throes of a mental breakdown? Was he making himself look like a messed-up person so he could justify the decision he had already made to kill himself? Or was he just really high?

I felt inadequate as a wife and petrified as a parent. What if our kids face similar struggles and don't feel comfortable confiding in me? That question left me with a terrible quandary. I had to decide: How much could I protect the man I still deeply loved while also looking out for my kids?

Those who approach us in public to praise Stephen or who post their cherished memories of him online while tagging us likely haven't considered this: Even though he made them feel seen and loved, his suicide caused unimaginable pain to me and my children. I harbored his secrets, not spilling the whole story to a soul even as people spoke to me about Stephen in the most glowing terms. People didn't know the whole scope. How could they? And yet as the months went on, it started to feel more and more dishonest not to acknowledge the signposts, however hidden from view, that might have led Stephen to that roadside motel just down the street from our house.

I would never let anyone talk badly about Stephen. But is it worth dwelling only on his best qualities, only on what he chose to show the world, when there are so many others potentially suffering in silence as he did? I want to give an honest accounting of what was going on—not to blame or shame anybody but to help other people who might see themselves or a loved one in Stephen. If you start seeing the signs I've described in someone else, ask questions. Be persistent. It can't hurt, and it just might save a life.

After Stephen's death, I heard from the parents of NFL defensive tackle Solomon Thomas, who lost their daughter, Solomon's big sister, to suicide in 2018. They reached out to offer their support, their sweet gesture harboring a sobering truth: I had become a member of a club to which nobody wants to belong. The Thomases, bless them, are among the small (but sadly growing) subset of people who've grappled with an unanswerable question: How does a loved one make the leap from temporary pain to this permanent solution?

In 2022, Stephen was one of 49,476 Americans to die by suicide, according to the Centers for Disease Control and Prevention's National Center for Health Statistics. When you consider how many grieving loved ones each of those other 49,475 left behind, the scope of the suffering, the vast reach of the ripple effects, becomes clearer. Whether or not people want to acknowledge it, suicide is part of the human condition. We can't *not* talk about it.

Picking up the pieces while upholding Stephen's legacy was exhausting. I was drained emotionally, physically—financially too. Neither

Stephen nor I had grown up with money. We hadn't had the good fortune to receive monetary support from our parents. As a result, we were united in our desire to give our children that luxury. We wanted them to have the leg up that we hadn't enjoyed. Building generational wealth was a priority for both of us. Creating and preserving assets to pass down to our kids was a regular topic of conversation. We were intentional about it.

In 2019, the same year we bought the family house in Encino, I also purchased a home in Utah with the idea that one day Weslie would inherit it. In 2022, Stephen and I bought two properties in Palm Springs that one day would go to Maddox and Zaia. The homes in Palm Springs needed work, which is why for much of 2022 I found myself making the 250-mile round-trip drive to the desert two or three times a week to meet with contractors and oversee renovations.

To my mild irritation, Stephen was disinterested in helping me. His heart just wasn't in it. Interior design had never been one of his strengths, so I didn't dwell much on his reluctance to get more involved. I interpreted his willingness to sit on the sidelines as a sign of his confidence in my ability to manage the projects. It's another one of those realities that hit differently after Stephen's death. Did he not care about those houses because he knew he wasn't going to stick around to behold the finished products?

His apathy toward the renovations solidifies in my mind that he had been thinking about leaving us for a while. The last couple of years that Stephen was alive, he was almost impatient about growing our financial portfolio. I can remember so many conversations where I'd say, "What's the rush? We have years and years and years to build our assets." It's so clear to me in retrospect that he was doing all he could to set us up for a secure future after he was gone. Yes, we were in good shape at the time of his suicide. But what he didn't consider was that the foundation that he had worked so hard to build for us would crumble after his death.

So many of our assets went with him. Stephen's name, for example, was on the property deeds for the Palm Springs houses. More than a year later, I was still mired in bureaucratic red tape as I sought to establish myself as the sole owner. As I went through the process of acquiring a clear title, I was paying mortgages on both houses, which became a heavy burden once I was having to pay all the bills. I'll have to sell the properties that Stephen had assumed would one day be passed on to the littles. They are two investments that became liabilities with Stephen's death, and while I'm not scared of starting over, I know that was never Stephen's wish for me. If he had known how much of our hard-earned money would go to pay lawyers' fees to clean up the mess he left me with, would it have made any difference?

I'd like to believe it would have. Stephen left me with double the work, double the noise, double the hardships, double the confusion—and half the household earnings. It's a misconception that I inherited Stephen's wealth. The reality is quite different. He had given away substantial sums of money to family and friends and spent recklessly on drugs and his weird art collections. The tax bill that he left me with for the year he died was $1 million. I'm not sure who was more distressed, me or the accountant who had to deliver the news.

Paying that debt depleted his accounts. This all came as a terrible surprise to me. We had always maintained separate bank accounts, and I had been under the impression that the arrangement was working just fine. He managed his income, and I managed mine, and we divvied up the bills. Easy-peasy. Or so I thought.

In truth, nothing was easy. I'm still jumping through endless bureaucratic hoops because Stephen didn't leave a will. We had started writing one at the suggestion of friends who are financial advisors. The sticking point on getting it done was that Stephen had not legally adopted Weslie, which made it more complicated to designate her as an heir. Stephen felt uncomfortable formally writing Weslie's biological father out of her life in a contract when she has a relationship with him. We decided to wait until Weslie became a legal adult before finalizing the paperwork. We weren't going anywhere. "What's a few more years?" we said.

I had to file a petition in the Superior Court of California in Los Angeles County to prove that I was married to Stephen to be able to claim his half of our joint estate. It was a technicality, but one that involved a lot of paperwork. But the absence of a will, it turned out, was the least of my concerns.

Stephen's suicide left me in breach of contract with our various business partners. I had no idea that suicide was considered a morality clause violation. So before Stephen had even been memorialized, I had to pull myself together and take meetings with our CPA and various business partners to determine which, if any, of our deals could be salvaged. And I had to manage all this without the person whose opinion and guidance I had come to rely on the most. His absence was the reason I was in this predicament.

Overnight, some companies completely cut ties with me. Others bowed out tactfully. I went from being a sought-after influencer to untouchable, collateral damage from Stephen's suicide. To those who declined to move forward with me, I had to be gracious and say, "I understand" when in reality I couldn't make the least bit of sense of anything that I was going through. God bless DICK's Sporting Goods, which was stuck with two apparel collections of ours that were tagged and ready to hit the sales floors but could no longer be sold. It cost the company millions of dollars in losses, and yet its executives stood behind me. Their continued support allowed me to pay bills and stay afloat during this tumultuous time.

I'm grateful, too, for HGTV, where Stephen and I had pending projects that included our own show, *Living the Dream*, revolving around first-time buyers, and a limited series, scheduled to go into production the following month, in which we were supposed to oversee the construction of a full-sized Malibu Barbie Dreamhouse. I had to relinquish my role as the host of the HGTV Barbie home makeover show to my dear friend Ashley Graham. But HGTV officials said they'd love to work with me again whenever I was ready, which I thought was a beautiful gesture.

Disney honored its contract to publish *Keep Dancing Through*, the children's book that Stephen and I had written about overcoming daily challenges. I told my contacts there to trust me on this: For the target audience, and our fans, this message never carried more relevance or resonance. The only thing my family or anybody who loved Stephen could do right then was keep dancing through. Thankfully, Disney agreed.

I had actually harbored some reservations about going ahead with publishing it. The thought occurred to me that the book might be better off as a keepsake for my children, a personal memento to remember their dad by. But I believed there was value in sharing its message with a broader audience. In 2024, the book came out and was well received—though I have to be honest, the press tour at times was triggering for me. Talking about a book that Stephen had helped create without him by my side was hard. My team wisely arranged for Weslie to accompany me to some of the events, which leavened my mood. We mixed in some fun with the business at hand, attending a Knicks and a Rangers game while we were in New York, for example, to take our minds off things.

I have a special bond with those who stuck by my side. We share a mutual respect that we survived these excruciatingly uncomfortable conversations to arrive at something that feels a lot like grace.

The passion project for which we had such high hopes is in limbo. There were so many business and brand relationships I had to reframe or restructure. I had to rebuild the foundation that Stephen and I had created while making myself available to my grieving kids and friends. There are shelved projects that I really hope can be resurrected, including one involving coffee.

Weirdly, the financial mess that was dumped in my lap after Stephen died provided a distraction from my grief. I literally couldn't afford not to be extra diligent about sorting out the mess. There were dire consequences for anything that was overlooked. I couldn't solely focus on mourning in those first few months because I was preoccupied with reworking contracts, rebuilding my business network, and getting my finances in order.

The surprises seemed never-ending. I realized we had no medical insurance because we had all been on Stephen's policy. At one point, it came to my attention that Stephen had neglected to pay our homeowner's insurance, forcing me to catch up on those bills. Almost two years later, I'm still in the trenches with a lot of it. For the longest time, I kept up Stephen's car payments. Magical thinking kept me from selling it until 2024: *What if I get rid of it and he comes back?*

Contrary to popular belief, I am not profiting significantly from his residuals, as Stephen's work primarily involved reality shows, where they are minimal. I claimed them mostly to ensure the taxes were properly paid. The bills he left for me were overwhelming. To pay them off I had to let go of our offices and a couple of valued members of our business team. Add to that the trauma of making call after call to close accounts or transfer them from Stephen's name to mine, of having to obtain and provide death certificates to bureaucrat after bureaucrat, and maybe it's clearer why I sometimes went out in the hot tub at night, far from the kids' bedrooms, and screamed at Stephen.

He used to say all the time, "Allison's strength is her strength." He even wrote it down in a few of the sweet notes we liked to leave for each other. In 2024, I appeared on Lewis Howes's podcast, and he showed me a clip from when Stephen had been his guest. Asked what he admired the most about me, Stephen replied, "If I had to choose one thing, man, it would be her constant, constant, undying ability to make it work. She has this ability to look at the cards she's been dealt and make it work."

I smiled at Lewis, whom I like and admire enormously. My exasperation was hardly his fault. But I couldn't shake the thought, *If I want someone to love me, and to stick around, do I have to be not so strong?* It's almost like my strength has been weaponized so that it has become my cross to bear.

I've lost plenty of sleep wondering, *If I was weaker, or if Stephen had perceived me as weaker, would he still be alive? Would he have refrained from killing himself if he believed I would have fallen apart?* Without question, I was the fixer in our relationship. Always solution-oriented, never self-pitying. Stephen knew I'd never let anyone talk bad about him. Did he also believe he could leave because I'd find a way to manage my grief and the grief of our children, figure it out, and find my way through? I remember one night screaming up at the stars, at Stephen, "*I know you'd still be here if you thought I'd fall apart!*"

I am certain that Stephen would never have left me if he didn't think I could take care of myself and the children. He never would have killed himself if he had suspected for one second that I would have been left so down and out that I would have become a distracted or neglectful parent. This is both a compliment and a curse. It's brutal, but it also gives me confidence that I can do this. I can carry on in his absence, and everything is going to be okay.

Since childhood, my journey has been marked by resilience. I was tough enough to make my own way in dance despite not having much money. I didn't let my traumatizing experience as a teen define me. Single motherhood didn't stop me. My resilience is undoubtedly a beautiful quality, yet there are moments when the expectation that I will find my way through whatever I'm facing can be overwhelming.

One evening in February 2023, I was outside gazing into the vastness of the night sky and talking to Stephen. "I forgive you," I whispered to him. "I can't sit with your pain and be a good mother. If this was your choice, I can't see that choice, I can't know that choice, but I forgive you for making that choice." Just saying those words was a liberating act that released a lot of psychic weight tethering me to the past.

I genuinely wished for Stephen the peace in death that eluded him in life. I walked back inside feeling lighter. It felt as if I had taken one small step toward grace and one giant leap toward healing.

Holding on to the what-ifs and whys is torturous because the only person capable of providing the answers is gone. Or does Stephen still exist, only in another realm, as he hypothesized during our Hawaii vacation?

A few months after I forgave Stephen, I agreed somewhat impetuously to a spiritual reading with a medium who came highly recommended by one of my dearest friends. "No pressure," he said, "but whenever you're ready, I think she could be helpful."

Since Stephen's death, so many people had recommended mediums or passed on the contact information of their psychic friends. Many healers reached out to me directly, eager to engage me in a reading. I was like, "No, no, no, no, no." It's not that I'm skeptical of these methods. I'll throw myself into spiritual pursuits with unbridled enthusiasm. I believe in energies and crystals and chakras and past lives and my dead spouse being able to communicate with me through a spiritual guide. For whatever reason, I just wasn't ready to receive the information. And then, suddenly, on a spring Monday, my friend reached out by text about connecting with his medium friend and something made me say, "Yes. How about this Friday?"

As I delved into this book project, I was so conflicted about how much to share about Stephen's final months. It's his story, after all, and he closely guarded it while he was alive. And now that he was no longer around to tell it, I'd been struggling with allowing myself to present sides of him that were a little scary. I wanted to be his protector, to take any negativity surrounding the circumstances of his death and absorb it so it wouldn't affect how people remembered him. One of the reasons I told the authorities there was no need for an autopsy was because I knew there'd be marijuana in his system, and I didn't want his drug use exposed to the wider world by TMZ or any other news outlet. By keeping to myself information that might prove helpful in understanding why he died, I hoped people would focus on how he lived.

I'm not sure what I wanted to gain by meeting with the medium. I was so nervous and scared, I almost canceled. At the time I wasn't fully sold on someone being able to communicate with the dead. I believe in spirits, but a little voice in my head said *I hope this person won't take advantage of my vulnerability.*

The reading took place remotely. I sat cross-legged on the floor of my bedroom, where I wouldn't be interrupted, and stared out the window while I waited for the phone call. I'm a big fan of healing crystals to release energy blockages—I think of them as plungers for the soul—so I made sure that I had a couple by my side. A movement outside caught my eye. It was a hummingbird, flapping its wings furiously. It felt like I was on the same vibrational frequency as that exquisite creature. I was also vaguely aware that hummingbirds are rich in symbolism, with some people believing that spotting them or dreaming about them can be interpreted as a sign that healing is imminent.

I didn't know how the call would proceed, but as soon as the medium started talking, we connected. We talked about life and love and kids like old friends. She had no idea I was writing this book. I didn't mention it, and my friend who connected us had never discussed it with her. So I sat up straighter when she said she knew that I was embarking on a new journey that really scared me. And even though I hadn't known how much I was free to share, Stephen wanted to make it clear that he's proud of me and he's giving his permission to share his other side because he believes it's important that he is seen—all of him.

It was Stephen's gift to make the people around him feel seen and heard. It was right there in the last interview we sat for together. Three weeks before Stephen killed himself, we appeared on Jennifer Hudson's talk show, and Stephen interrupted her gushing about us—"One of the cutest couples on TikTok! . . . The energy is amazing!"—to rally the audience behind Jennifer. "Isn't she doing great?" he said. "Let me give you your flowers." Now he was telling me, essentially, no more deflection. Stephen said that he knew I was protecting him, like I always have, but I don't need to hold on to his life for him anymore. He's okay with people knowing the *whole* him.

My relief was palpable. Romanticizing someone who has taken their life is dangerous. No one choosing this path ought to be glorified. It's possible to hate the act and have great love and empathy for the person who made that decision. It's okay to be extremely upset with Stephen while still greatly admiring him. Those emotions can coexist.

I can be mad at Stephen because I miss him. I can be mad at him for not telling me where he was that last night. I can be mad at him because he left me to raise three kids alone and it's freaking hard. Mad at him for leaving me career-wise because we had so much going for us. Mad at him because we loved each other so much. I was so in love with him, and I don't know if I'll ever deserve that love again because I got to have this big, beautiful, dramatic, dizzying love, and look how it turned out.

Mad at him because I had to take off my beautiful wedding ring. It served as a constant reminder that he had decided to leave me and the children instead of honoring the vow we made to grow old together. But mostly, I can be mad at him because when he decided to put an end to his pain, he couldn't have been thinking clearly about our amazing kids. I worry about them so much, and I'm mad at him for not considering how much they'd worry about me with him gone.

CHAPTER 14

LEAN ON ME

We had been a family of five, and now we are four. Our new configuration is jarring to some people. Once we emerged from our hibernation and resumed our day-to-day lives, it was as if every time we stepped out in public, people saw a ghost. Sometimes that phantom presence was Stephen. Sometimes it was someone's loved one who had died by suicide. It didn't matter where I went or who I was with. I got stopped by people who wanted to share some memory of Stephen or talk about someone they loved who had killed themselves.

It was intense. I'd be filling my tank at the gas station and other customers would look at me with pity. I'd pick up dry cleaning and be greeted by sad faces. At the grocery store, my arrival would trigger whispers among other shoppers. There were so many tears, not all of them mine. I told the kids it was going to be like this until people grew accustomed to seeing us out and about. So as uncomfortable as it was at first, we couldn't retreat. We had to work through the discomfort and awkwardness.

One of our first forays in public as a family was a shopping trip to Trader Joe's. Zaia was riding in the shopping cart that I was pushing while Maddox was beside me, holding my hand. Weslie was also with us. As soon as we entered the store, shoppers in the vicinity did double takes. Two women, both strangers, approached and gave me hugs. A third woman, with her elderly mother in tow, came up to us. The daughter told me her father—her mother's husband—had died by suicide. My eyes welled with tears. "I'm so, so sorry," I said. Inside, I was thinking, Suicide *is an awfully big word for Maddox's ears.*

As if reading my mind, Maddox squeezed my hand three times. It was our secret code for *I. Love. You.* I looked down at him and he nodded solemnly at me as if to say, *You've got this, Mom.* My kids have handled interactions like this with unfortunate grace. I say unfortunate because I wish they didn't have to be in this place.

We've had a few excursions to restaurants that have not gone well, as is bound to happen when your dining companions include a hyperactive eight-year-old and a bossy four-year-old. At one meal, Maddox and Zaia engaged in a crayon-throwing contest. At another, they spit their food at each other. I trust any parent of small children will recognize these behaviors. The only way I can teach my kids to act civilly in public is to take them out in public, but the spotlight we're under is such that their age-appropriate acting out is spun as my fatherless children's unraveling.

Protecting my kids from curious adults and unkind peers has proved an impossible task. We were still sequestered in our house when I got an agonizing reminder of how little control I have over our circumstances. I invited one of Maddox's friends from his first-grade class to our house for a playdate. The boy was accompanied by his father. As the grown-ups, which included my nanny and her husband, talked inside, I happened to glance outside at the patio in time to see the little boy whispering something in Maddox's ear. I saw Maddox recoil. From the horror written all over his face, I knew exactly what had just transpired.

I made an excuse to cut the playdate short. Once our guests were gone, I asked Maddox what his friend had whispered to him. "He said my dad shot himself in the face," Maddox said. "Is that true? And how would he know? Why would he know?" Poor Maddox. He was devastated. The revelation shattered the truth as he had conjured it in his imagination—that his dad had gone into space and lost his helmet, and that's why he now resides in the stars.

I made clear that I didn't think his friend should have known the details of what happened. I said it was incredibly mean of him to say what he did. I told Maddox that I absolutely had planned to tell him what happened one day, maybe not using quite the same language that the little boy did. But now that he knew, it was important for him to understand that what Daddy did had nothing to do with him. It had nothing to do with any of us. I explained that Daddy was really confused and was going through a terribly tough time. And though he is not with us like before, he still loves us and is watching over us.

The conversation just about broke me. Maddox lost his innocence at six. He can never get that back.

Around this same time, I was walking hand in hand with Maddox in our neighborhood, just blocks from our house, when a man on the opposite sidewalk began belligerently screaming the N-word at us. He crossed the street, and I tightened my grip on Maddox's hand and whispered, "Come on. Come on. It's okay." Maddox was confused. He had never heard that word before.

He looked up at me with his sweet eyes and asked me what the word meant. I had tears in my eyes as I explained to him that it's a crude description for people with his beautiful skin color. I was seething, but not at the man, who passed us on the sidewalk without incident. In that moment I was so upset at Stephen. He *knew* Maddox would face racism. I thought, *How could you leave Maddox to navigate this kind of stuff without your guidance?* I'm going to do my best to help him through these situations, but I'm no substitute for Stephen.

After the incident with his classmate, I researched other schools where Maddox could resume first grade. The one I chose, which he's attending now, is nurturing and attuned to its students' emotional lives. He couldn't have ended up at a better place. I knew it was perfect when, during the school tour, I came upon a bulletin board of many colors, with each hue representing an emotion ranging from sadness to happiness and just about everything in between. Each student has their name written on a popsicle stick, and every morning they place their stick on the emotion that best describes their mood that day. If another student or teacher sees that someone is angry or sad, they make the effort to reach out and see if that child wants to talk about it.

I frequently field questions about which words are appropriate to be used around my children. What *should* people say to them, or around them, about what happened? I'm moved by the thoughtfulness behind the questions, but I have no definitive answers. I feel the weight of being the one looked to for guidance when in truth I am wandering lost in a maze of emotions myself. There are no GPS directions for this journey. I feel as if I'm expected to lead the way when I'm stumbling through the brush, clearing a path as I muddle through. Processing my grief while simultaneously serving as the receptacle of my children's is a destabilizing experience. I'm not sure I have the necessary tools and knowledge. I simply want them to be okay, yet the way forward is hazy. Maybe when I've healed more, the path will become clearer. I can only hope so.

Zaia appears largely unfazed. She has expressed curiosity more than anything. In the beginning, she asked constantly, "When's Daddy coming home?"

I'd answer, "Remember, baby, Daddy's not coming home because he's watching us from the sky."

Eventually, she stopped asking. Several months later, Zaia came to me and, out of the blue, posed a different question that made it clear that she understood more than anybody knew: "Why did Dad die?"

"His brain was really hurting him," I replied, "and he couldn't fix it."

I'm so thankful that she comes to me with these questions. I want so much to be her rock, her hero. If nothing else, I want her to know that I'll never leave her. If Zaia has more questions about her dad as she gets older, even if I don't have the perfect words, she'll be able to turn to her sister and brother. She has aunts and uncles and cousins who will always be there for her too.

We get the comment a lot about how lucky we are that there is so much video of Stephen so the kids, especially Zaia, can remember him. And while that's true, consider that the only memories Zaia will have of Stephen will be shaped by the stories we tell her about those moments captured on film. Sad, isn't it?

Zaia seems to have adjusted to our new normal better than the rest of us. My precious four-year-old has taught me so much about boundaries. We'll be cuddling on the couch, watching a movie with our treats and popcorn and the whole nine yards. One minute she'll say, "Oh, Mommy, I love you," and the next minute she'll suddenly announce, "I need alone time," and off she goes. She has been known to take visitors' hands and walk them to the front door when she thinks it's time for them to go. Imagine being okay letting people know when you're done, when you've had enough!

I lean into the idea that parenting isn't a one-way street. It's not my way or the highway. These tiny humans we bring into the world can teach us a thing or two, creating a cycle where they learn from you, then turn around and help you learn something.

I thought of my precious baby girl the other night when I hosted a party and people stayed until four in the morning. I wanted to be in bed at 11 p.m., but I'm a people pleaser, so I did nothing. After midnight I found myself wishing I could channel Zaia and simply take my guests' hands, one by one, and lead them to the front door.

I can appreciate how hard it would have been for another people pleaser, Stephen, to ask for help. I can follow his train of thought even if I cannot get on board with it: If he needed help, who would be there for us? I can't rewrite Stephen's history, but I do have it within my power to armor my kids against shame or depression by teaching them that it's okay to be vulnerable.

To accomplish that, I first had to stop masking my feelings when I was overwhelmed, angry, or sad. I couldn't very well sell my kids on the importance of expressing their uncomfortable emotions when I would save my ugly crying for the shower or lock myself in the closet to scream it out. How could I expect them to come to me and share how they're feeling when I wasn't letting them see me being vulnerable?

I prided myself on being a tough cookie around them. Not because I was trying to be a superhero like Stephen; I just didn't want my kids to be burdened by my emotions. I was the adult in the room, after all. My well-being was not their concern, whereas their emotional stability is one of my main responsibilities. The first time I broke down and ugly cried in front of them, right after Stephen's death, was the first step toward establishing an open, two-way line of communication in which Weslie, Maddox, and Zaia feel free to lean on me (or one another) when they're not okay.

Who knew that being emotionally open with my children was a lesson I desperately needed? Not this self-starting, solution-seeking striver who prided herself on taking lemons and making the world's best lemonade served up with a sprig of mint and paper cocktail parasols. I'd always aimed to lead by example, especially when it came to chasing dreams. Now it was time for me to show them the importance of being fearless with their emotions.

What we were going through was hard, I told my kids, but we were going to get through it because we'd figure it out together. We had one another and an amazing support system to lean on. Not everybody is so fortunate. And if I was occasionally the one who needed picking up, so be it.

One afternoon Weslie returned from school to find me in the back-yard curled up in a ball. I was clutching a wand lighter and bawling. I didn't hold back my sobs, even after Weslie came up from behind and wrapped her arms around me.

"I don't know how to turn on the outside grill," I said.

But that wasn't the half of it. The sight of the grill called to mind a memory that triggered a flash of insight. Stephen was fond of saying that his stepfather taught him how to barbecue. In truth, Stephen was not exactly George Foreman around a grill. He was unsure of himself when he was at the controls. I had never picked up on that contradiction until I went outside that day to light the barbecue, and then it hit me.

What did it mean that Stephen repeated a story about his stepfather that obviously wasn't true? What did he gain or unwittingly reveal by doing so? Only since his death have I realized that Stephen lied to me about all kinds of things, big and small, for so long, and I had no idea. If only I had recognized the pattern, maybe I could have asked him the right questions that would have sparked a revelatory conversation. I will forever feel so sad and so mad at myself for not seeing the lies.

So I wasn't really bawling because I didn't know how to work the grill. From the fierceness of Weslie's hug, I suspect that she intuited as much. "It's okay," she said soothingly. "We'll watch a YouTube video and learn together." And that's what we did. I felt bad that she saw me so completely undone, but I was grateful for her presence.

I struggle with Weslie wanting to mother me. I have visions of her seeking out a therapist down the road to unpack all the issues that resulted from the excessive responsibility and emotional burden she shouldered from being parentified. However, our therapist tamped down my fears by noting that Weslie's support and protection of me are vital components of her healing journey. Doctor-patient privilege prevents her from sharing with me what she and Weslie talk about, but she did allow, "You two are like the same human."

I laughed because I knew exactly what she meant. Though our personalities are different—Weslie's an assertive Gemini, while I'm a more composed Aquarius—we complement each other. I take great comfort in our deep connection. I was so young when she was born, barely twenty, so I feel as if we have grown up together. I've always been transparent with her about my failings. I've emphasized that we are both students of life, learning together. Her emotional maturity continually astounds me, and I'm impressed with her innate ability to see the bigger picture.

It took months, but one day Weslie and I got to reminiscing about the piles of clutter that Stephen habitually left on his chair at the kitchen table. We burst into laughter—then stopped. Was laughter an appropriate response? Was it a betrayal of Stephen to enjoy a lighthearted moment at his expense? We ultimately agreed that it was all right. Stephen would have wanted us to have light hearts and embrace beautiful memories. Everything shifted for me in that instant. Stephen's absence was permanent, but our grief didn't have to be. Life was still to be lived and enjoyed.

I've learned so much from Weslie. She is my rock, and vice versa. It saddens me that I haven't been able to do more to protect her through what happened. It was challenging for her to resume in-person classes at her Catholic high school. The drop-off zone was the last place she saw Stephen, and his final words to her are a triggering memory she has had to face day after day. The paparazzi initially followed her, adding to her distress. Fortunately, the school provided excellent support through counseling and caring teachers. I really cannot say enough about how the people at her school have looked out for her.

Her return coincided with the death of a beloved teacher, and in one of her first days back a memorial mass was held. Weslie was given the option not to attend. She expressed the desire to pay her last respects alongside the rest of the student body only to experience a panic attack. A couple of friends, a teacher, and a counselor walked outside with her until the symptoms subsided. The same people were there for her several months later when three students at another private high school in the area—a sophomore, a junior, and a senior—died by suicide in a seven-month span in 2023, leading teachers at her school to start a dialogue about mental health.

The kids were around her age, and Weslie, never one to relish being the center of attention, found her classmates turning to her and asking, "What do we do? How do you handle it?" Imagine being fifteen and returning to school to regain some semblance of normalcy only to find you've become the authority on suicide among your classmates.

Weslie has handled it with remarkable strength. There have been tearful moments and ample trials and tribulations, but she has coped admirably. Have there been times when Weslie has had to take a mental health day? Yes. I've called the school and said, "Hey, Weslie's having a really hard day today," and everybody works with us. They have been so patient. It's challenging enough to be a teenager, but to have to go through this stage while also processing such a public trauma could break a less resilient person.

Surrounded by a supportive network of friends and teachers, Weslie is on an admirable journey of growth and self-improvement. As I write this, she is finishing her sophomore year, during which she dived into honors classes and pursued a beauty school certification with an eye toward opening a salon tailored for teenagers. When I was her age, I had dance to anchor me during the rocky times. Dance gave me stability and direction. I do worry about Weslie because she hasn't locked into her passion. (I can hear her now: *Mother, I'm only sixteen. You were the weird one to know what you wanted to do with your life at that age.*) I keep telling her to live as big a life as she can. What that will look like, only time will tell.

But I will tell you this: I worry a lot less than I used to. I've changed my whole trajectory with Weslie since Stephen's death. I want to push her to be the best person she can be for herself, but not at the expense of her mental health. I now tell her all the time, "Your well-being matters more than anything." I encourage her to pace herself. She shouldn't feel compelled to keep up with my frenetic life. (Then again, *I* shouldn't feel compelled to keep up with my frenetic life.)

I introduced Weslie to dance classes when she was little, much younger than I had been when I started. But I could tell early on it wasn't going to be her thing. It had nothing to do with her talent—and everything to do with mine. She'd tag along with me to dance conventions and people would enthuse, "Oh, you're going to be a pro dancer like your mom." Weslie grew tired of being compared to me and quit. "I don't like it anymore," she said at the time. "It's too much pressure."

That conversation has stuck with me, which is why I shudder every time Maddox is asked, "Are you going to follow your daddy into dancing?" The question, however innocent and well-intentioned, is awfully heavy for a child to process. It was one thing for people to wonder if Weslie would follow in my choreographed steps, but to ask a child to keep alive their dead father's memory is too much. I signed up Maddox for baseball the summer after Stephen died and people said to him, "Oh, your daddy loved baseball." Actually, he didn't! Stephen recalled standing in the outfield humming to himself because he was so bored.

People are just trying to be supportive. I get it. I simply want to point out how confusing it can be for a child to constantly be compared to a father who died in shame, as Stephen's suicide note made clear. My kids already have to deal with a lot, and it's deepening the trauma to expect every choice Stephen's children make to be a reflection of him. People say, "Stephen would be so proud of your grades!" or "Math is your favorite subject? Stephen loved math too." I understand that maybe some people feel closer to Stephen if they're around his kids, but please know that my children do not exist to help anybody heal. Their purpose in life is not to carry on Stephen's legacy. It's to create their own.

Yes, Maddox can dance. He's such a little performer. So is Zaia. But at the end of the day, I don't want my children to feel any pressure to be anything but the best version of themselves.

It's imperative for their overall well-being that Stephen's suicide does not become the defining event of their lives. I want them to view their father's life as a beautiful chapter that ended abruptly. I want them to carry on knowing that they have their own stories to write.

I often find myself being compared to Vanessa Bryant, whose husband, Kobe, a retired basketball superstar and Oscar-winning documentarian, died at age forty-one in a helicopter crash along with one of their children, leaving her to raise their remaining three daughters by herself. Vanessa has reached out to me since Stephen's death, and one of these days I'm going to seek out her wise counsel. She's a beautiful spirit whom I greatly admire.

I'm asked why I don't connect with companies and individuals to find ways to honor the life and legacy of my late husband like Vanessa has done (and beautifully so). I'm asked why I am no longer wearing my wedding ring as she is still known to do. The answer is straightforward: Kobe didn't voluntarily leave Vanessa. He passed away in a tragic accident. By taking his own life, Stephen made his death and legacy a profoundly complex situation.

I started the Move with Kindness Foundation to honor Stephen's memory. I can't wake up every day thinking, *How will I live my life for Stephen?* The foundation gave me a focused place to honor him and keep his legacy alive by spreading love and mental health awareness. Through partnerships with the National Alliance on Mental Illness (NAMI) and OUR HOUSE Grief Support Center, we are actively increasing awareness of mental health issues while providing resources for children, teens, and adults who are mourning the loss of loved ones.

A significant criticism I've faced revolves around my decision not to constantly share loving memories of, and tributes to, Stephen on social media. I've been labeled as selfish for choosing not to do so. The pressure to continuously honor him, particularly through social media, fails to take into account my children's reality. It fails to consider their grief. If I were to portray Stephen as the best father in every social post, highlighting only the positive without acknowledging the hurt he caused us, it could inadvertently make my children feel responsible for his pain.

They're already grappling with the trauma of questioning whether he truly loved them, whether it was their fault that he was so despondent. My kids will inevitably face anger, a sense of being robbed of a father, and long-lasting triggers and trauma due to his actions. So if I've stopped posting photos of our family that include Stephen, I hope people will understand. And if they don't, well, I've accepted that I'll never be able to meet everyone's expectations. Whether I like it or not, I'll always be subjected to comparisons and judgments. That's my reality now. To counter the outside voices, I've developed a mantra that is my new superpower: *I'm sorry if my life offends you, but I won't change it for you. You don't get to write my story. I'm the author of my story.*

Don't let my children's smiling faces at red-carpet events or at Disneyland or Universal Studios fool you. They are still hurting. In the winter of 2024, the littles and I were soaking in our backyard jacuzzi, which has become one of our favorite nighttime activities. Zaia pointed at the stars, and I said, "Yes. There's Daddy. He's in the sky looking down on us."

Maddox climbed out of the water and sat on the edge. He is usually a cutup, like his father, but his body language was very tense. Something clearly was bothering him.

"What's going on?" I asked. "You can tell me."

"No, I can't," he said. "You'll be mad if I tell you."

"I promise you, I'm not going to be mad at you no matter what you say," I said. "Can I just ask you some questions?"

Maddox nodded.

"Does it have to do with Daddy?"

Another nod.

"Does it make you sad?"

"Yeah."

"Does it make you angry?"

"Yeah," he said. "I'm really angry at Dad. I know I'm not supposed to be, but I'm really mad at him."

"Oh, baby," I said, "I want you to know that I'm still angry at Dad too. Why are you mad at him?"

"Because he's not here for me or you or Zaia or Weslie."

"You're right," I said. "You have every right to be mad at him. That's okay. On a scale of one to ten, how angry are you?"

"I can't say."

"Okay," I said. "On a scale of one to ten, how much do you miss him?"

"Ten."

"How much do you love him?"

"To the moon and back and the whole universe," he said.

Sweet little Maddox. He was so scared to say what was in his heart. It made me so sad, but I was also extraordinarily proud of him. It was a breakthrough for my son, the comedian, to give voice to such heavy emotions. It gave me hope that he'll be okay.

Stephen educated me so much about being a Black male. As a boy, he said he was taught to never display weakness, never to let his emotions show. To buck up and be brave. I don't think Stephen was being honest about how much, even as a grown man, he was still invested in acing those lessons. If he hadn't kept his sadness and anger hidden, if he had been able to express it like his eight-year-old son, where might he, and we, be today?

And what was Zaia doing during this whole conversation? She kept extending one arm to slap the water and splash Maddox while she giggled. I had to keep pushing her hand down while not taking my eyes off Maddox.

The steps of this new dance I'm choreographing on the fly are intricate, almost impossible to teach or master. Though I will say, it got easier after a change of venue.

CHAPTER 15

HOME SWEET HOME

Some decisions are too momentous to make alone. One of the things that was so wonderful about being married to Stephen was that I knew I could always lean on him for advice. But his absence—or rather, his shadow presence—led to the greatest conundrum I would face in our family's first year without him.

Our Encino home had been Stephen's refuge, and his influence pervaded every art-adorned wall, every piece of furniture, every room. In the months prior to his death, we had been canvassing real estate listings for a place with a more expansive backyard to accommodate what we had hoped would be more kids and pets. In the immediate aftermath of his suicide, it felt right to remain rooted in place. The house became so much more than our mailing address. It was a museum that preserved all our memories of Stephen.

My friend T.J., a real estate agent, told me that whenever I was ready to move, he was at my service. I thanked him, but my first thought was *I don't know if we'll ever want to change houses*. We found solace in the familiar surroundings. With everything the children had lost, I thought it was a prudent move to stay put. Why uproot Maddox and Zaia from the only house they'd ever known at a time when their lives had already been turned upside down?

We had our nightly ritual of sitting in the hot tub, under the stars, and conversing with Stephen. We could feel his electromagnetic force field in the sky and inside in the lights that flickered in response to questions and comments we'd pose to him. It was a metaphysical connection that we cherished—until we didn't.

After a while, there was a palpable shift in the house's energy. Maddox and Zaia, who rarely bickered, suddenly started behaving very disagreeably toward each other. And as wild as this sounds, the electricity became moody, acting up without rhyme or reason. Weslie or I would walk into a room, turn on the light, and . . . nothing. While visiting my mom in Utah, Weslie and I noticed that the lights flickered whenever either of us was in the bathroom. But when mom went in there, the lights worked perfectly. I know it sounds wild, but it was obvious to me Stephen was trying to communicate with us.

At some point I began to feel spooked by the bed that Stephen and I had shared. It became a nightmare to sleep in it. I wouldn't touch his side except to change the sheets. I could still retrieve my clothes from the walk-in closet that we had both used as long as I didn't look at Stephen's side. But after a while, just being in that space became triggering.

I started noticing that the kids also had their own avoidance issues. There were certain chairs that Stephen favored that everyone steered clear of because the memory of him sitting there when we played cards or a board game was so strong. Weslie tiptoed around the office that Stephen and I had shared.

Then there were the signs. I started finding stray feathers, which, according to a book I read, represented messages from the deceased. Was Stephen trying to tell me to let go of the house so we could soar instead of feeling stuck?

I had asked Stephen to let me know that he was watching over us. He was almost too vigilant. After a while his presence became overwhelming, and I had to ask him to stop. Weslie and I would have tons of dreams about him, all of which were eerily realistic; Weslie would often see him sitting on the edge of her bed.

We were slowly healing on the inside, but the exterior symbol of our family—our home—was sagging under the weight of an astral asbestos. The neighborhood also had taken on a haunted quality, with memories of Stephen lurking around every corner. I had to drive past the Oak Tree Inn, where he died, every time I went to the grocery store, the post office, the dry cleaners, our preferred big-box store, my favorite restaurants, or the juice bar that Stephen and I loved. It was sheer torture. I'd stare straight ahead and keep on driving, as if I could make the motel disappear by ignoring it.

One day, hand on heart, that motel will cease to exist. I don't know how, and I don't care how much money it costs, but my goal is to buy it and tear it down. Maybe build in its place a beautiful dance studio. I need to change that space's energy.

With summer on its way out, I decided that maybe it was time for us, too, to make our exit. I floated the idea of moving to Weslie. I asked her to be brutally honest. Her answer was unambiguous. "Mother, we've been ready for months," she said. "We've all been concerned that *you* weren't ready."

When I informed Maddox and Zaia that we were going to find another house to live in, they said, "Yay! That will be fun!"

With Labor Day and the start of the 2023–24 school year fast approaching, I phoned T.J. and told him I thought we were ready to start considering a move. If I had waffled any more, he could have poured maple syrup over me.

"Baby, I got you," he said. "What are you thinking?"

I said that *if* we were to move, I wanted to stay in Encino, close to Stephen's energy but also close enough to Maddox's school that I could continue to walk him there and back.

"Are you sure?" T.J. said. He explained that he had found a home that was perfect for me. It was on the border of Studio City and North Hollywood, so a good half hour's drive in normal traffic from our old neighborhood.

That didn't sound ideal, but T.J. was persistent. "I know your personality, and I know your style, and I'm telling you, there is a home that is *your* home," he said. "I've been wanting you to see it."

I made no promises but agreed to look at the house, a six-bedroom, seven-bath modern farmhouse, the next day. T.J. was right. I instantly fell in love with it. The property was lighter and airier than our Encino home, with twelve-foot vaulted-beam ceilings and sliding glass pocket doors to the backyard to create an indoor-outdoor living space. My eyes welled with tears as I took in the custom-made oak cabinets in the kitchen, which gave off such a warm, healing vibe, and the pendant lights over the quartzite counters.

The lines of the house were so clean—much more my style than the house in Encino, though the bones of both places were similar. It's a lot of house—I'll grant you that. And an argument could have been made that downsizing would have made more practical sense. But after my childhood spent constantly moving to ever more diminished spaces, it was important to me that my children didn't sense a shift in their standard of living. I would do whatever it took so that my kids didn't feel house insecure like I had. They had already lost so much. I couldn't bear the thought of them having to downgrade their way of life.

For the first time in months, I was able to deeply exhale. I was surprised by that because I hadn't even been conscious of holding my breath in the old house. Before I had even toured the upstairs, I informed T.J. that this was my new house. Within four days of first laying eyes on the place, I made an offer, contingent on the sale of the Encino property, and it was accepted. I had just one itsy-bitsy request: Could we close the sale in three weeks so we could move in before the children started back at school? Okay, it was an impossible ask. But somehow T.J., working with my team, managed to pull it off.

I had to sell our other home and pack up our belongings, ideally without the press getting a whiff of the move that was underfoot. The last thing the kids needed was to have their photographs taken as we pulled out of the driveway for the last time. I didn't want to have to explain the move to anybody. I didn't want friends or family members trying to talk me out of it. I withdrew from people, not to avoid having to talk but because there was so much that needed to get done, I didn't have time to answer phone calls or reply to texts. When I failed to respond, people freaked out. They read all kinds of things into my silence, mostly that I was in a dark place.

Quite the opposite was true. I was the boss, the move was one of my first major executive decisions since Stephen's death, and I wanted to show that I was handling things like a competent adult. Yet it was overwhelming. I felt stressed out most of the time, but also empowered. With a lot of help, I pulled it off. The successful execution of this milestone event became a harbinger of my and my kids' fresh start.

Korinne, my assistants Adrienne and Kat, and I served as the de facto moving team. I must say I don't think women in general get enough credit for how tough and resilient we are. In the movies, men are always saving women from distress. That has just not been my experience. My assistants are my sheroes. All the women I know are strong. They aren't relying on any man to save them. In fact, they're the ones holding things together. More movies need to be made about female heroines swooping in to save the day. I'm just saying.

Going all in on the fresh-start theme, we rented a dumpster and took a symbolic step in our healing journey by dividing our belongings into four piles: donate, discard, store, or take. As I started sifting through the past decade of my life, I realized there was relatively little that I wished to keep. The fabric in furniture holds memories (and energy), clothing holds memories (and energy), the wall art and sculptures hold memories (and energy). They were all cool memories and calming energies curdled by Stephen's abandonment of us. I had no desire, for example, to bring to the new house any of the old outfits that I had worn in our annual family portraits. Once upon a time they had been among my favorites, but now I knew they'd likely just make me sad.

I would pack boxes for Korinne or Kat to haul to Goodwill or our storage unit, which I couldn't bring myself to visit. It contained too many memories, like the statue of the embracing couple that Stephen and I had bought in Laguna Beach. One day I might decide to reintroduce it to the house, but probably not anytime soon. The act of purging material belongings became a critical part of our family's emotional recovery. We tossed old towels, toothbrushes, sheets, pillows, and clothing. It was one slam dunk after another, items that we heaved from Weslie's second-floor bedroom window toward the dumpster below.

Shoes associated with specific events and other sentimental items were donated, but not before we fondly relived the memories. Unexpected discoveries, like a forgotten playbill from a theater production in New York, surfaced, triggering long-buried emotions. What to do with the dining table, around which we sat night after night sharing and shaping so many stories? After much agonizing, we decided to store it. A gray plaid blanket that Stephen loved even though it failed to cover his entire body, so his size 13 feet stuck out? Discarded, but not before Weslie and I shared a laugh at the image that was still so fresh in our minds.

The decluttering was hard but cathartic. I trusted my intuition. I realized that I could navigate through this emotional minefield and make difficult decisions, which was empowering.

I saved some of Stephen's many sneakers and hoodies for Maddox when he's older. I put aside others to give to Stephen's brothers and friends. The black swivel office chair that Stephen would wheel around went into storage. My assistants sold a few items online. Letting go of sentimental items was excruciating, but I discovered that preserving memories doesn't require clinging to physical possessions. We can tap into cherished moments without having the corresponding memento. Letting go does not mean forgetting.

A few items of Stephen's I kept for myself. His wedding ring. One of the many notes he left on the kitchen counter or tucked into my suitcase or placed on my pillow, beautiful messages composed in his scratchy, all-but-indecipherable handwriting. I never thought I'd say it, but I miss his messy script. A beaded bracelet that is identical to one that I have. His rosary (I don't know the backstory behind it, but he had it for as long as I knew him). His journals. A half-empty bottle of his Tom Ford cologne.

A couple of hoodies and a handful of T-shirts—the same design but in different colors.

Weslie took two of the T-shirts for herself. She was beside herself after she put one in the wash and it came out with bleach blots. She came running into my room clutching the shirt and crying that she had ruined it. Consoling her, I said I had another one I could give her.

Despite our precautions to keep the move under wraps, a story was published that divulged every detail of it. The invasion of privacy was a bummer, but I was surprised by how many people rallied around our right to personal space.

The kids hadn't seen the new house before we relocated. I was worried that one or all of them would be let down or feel disappointed by the neighborhood or struggle to acclimate to their new surroundings. If anyone was unhappy, the move never would have worked. But I need not have worried. They were all in on this new adventure. Their happiness was palpable. They were so excited.

They raced up the stairs to claim their own bedrooms. Each child found a space that perfectly reflected their tastes and personalities. Weslie was drawn to a room decorated for a teenage girl, so much so that she didn't change a thing. Maddox, who was learning to skateboard at the time, jumped on the bedroom with framed art of a Black skateboarder in flight. He liked the picture so much, I made sure the artwork was conveyed. Zaia, who loves animals, picked a room with framed art of a dog.

As we settled into our new space, it was as if we all had been unchained from a ghost. Liberated. It hadn't been apparent until then how much the old house had been hindering our healing. Everyone felt lighter and more at peace in the new house. It became our sacred place. The move drew us even closer as a family because we each had to commit to it and trust one another that it was the right thing to do. Was it ever! The benefits extended well beyond having a bigger space. The new house brought us more joy, more happiness, more clarity. It inspired new conversations. New transparency. New traditions.

The move cut Weslie's commute to school in half (and then some). I drove her most days but didn't continue the habit that she and Stephen had of stopping for a breakfast sandwich on the way. As a family, we still go to Starbucks on occasion, but whether it's due to a maturing palate or a triggering memory, Weslie has changed her drink order from a sickly sweet latte that contained four pumps of this syrup and three pumps of that syrup to a matcha green tea latte.

I am a big believer in family traditions. They strengthen bonds and foster memories. One of the things that Stephen found the most attractive about me was my enthusiastic embrace of established practices and my readiness to adopt new customs—probably because he said he grew up without any. This new chapter calls for fresh traditions—which is not to say I've thrown out all the old ones.

With Weslie, I've maintained our tradition of mother-and-daughter manicures, and I recently introduced a new one. Every month I send her a bouquet of flowers with an enclosed card containing an inspirational message or a silly inside joke. She collects the cards, which warms my heart. My motivation for sending the flowers is that I suspect that she, like me, will have daddy issues after everything that has gone down. I can't take the place of her father or Stephen, but I can let her know, unequivocally, that she is deserving of being loved and pampered. My message to her is to hold out for a partner who will give her the attention she deserves.

I shoot hoops with Maddox in the morning and read to Zaia at night. I've started taking Maddox and Zaia separately for ice cream at one of two shops near our new home. We also walk to the park nearby. Maddox is a huge Spider-Man fan. Not coincidentally, so is Zaia. They pack their Spider-Man costumes in their backpacks when they go to the park in case they need to protect the neighborhood.

We're a big costume family. When Stephen was alive, Halloween was a huge deal in our house. We'd have a sit-down meeting at the dining room table and each family member would write down a costume idea on a slip of paper and place it in a jar. We'd draw one of the slips and we would all outfit ourselves according to that theme—think the Addams family or Harry Potter. If someone was adamantly opposed to the motif, we'd do two themed costumes.

On Halloween night, we'd take the kids around the neighborhood as a family. Even Weslie, once she reached her teenage years, continued to participate and bring her friends along, some of whom would also outfit themselves according to our chosen theme. Our approach has always been the more the merrier. The first Halloween without Stephen, Weslie and I took the littles trick-or-treating, but no one expressed any interest in the themed costumes, so we didn't wear matching outfits. After a year's hiatus, we definitely plan to bring back the tradition in 2024.

But other cherished rituals fell by the wayside. We used to have a family tradition of birthday cookie cakes. The kids clamored for them. They would look forward to a gooey Mrs. Fields chocolate chip cookie cake with their name and "Happy Birthday" written across the face in icing. Three months after Stephen died, Maddox turned seven. He did not ask for a cookie cake. Two months after that, Weslie celebrated her fifteenth birthday. She didn't ask for one either.

But we still had a great time celebrating these occasions, which provided us pockets of joy amid so much sorrow.

As Stephen's birthday week approached in September, we couldn't escape the reminders. People posted about it on social media and tagged us, which upset Weslie, who found it triggering to see Stephen praised as the best father and someone who embodied love and light when we were still dealing with the fallout from what he'd done.

We heard from people who wanted to join us in mourning on his birthday. They no doubt meant well, but it was not helpful. The best comparison I can make is when people descend in droves on soup kitchens to volunteer around Thanksgiving because that's when they're thinking about the needy. But the rest of the time they're too preoccupied with their own lives, as if people aren't in need of food the other eleven months of the year.

People wanted to share in our pain on Stephen's birthday, not realizing we had been marinating in it all year. I heard from friends who said, "You have no idea how much I'm hurting, Allison," expecting me to help them navigate their discomfort. We couldn't meet these people where they were in their grieving because it would only drag us all back into that dark space. Some of Stephen's family members celebrated "29 Days of Stephen" throughout September, a takeoff on *The Ellen DeGeneres Show*'s "12 Days of Christmas," which Weslie found deeply unsettling. She expressed that her father is not a holiday. I explained that everyone grieves and heals in their own way and acknowledged the beauty of their tribute.

How should we commemorate the occasion? I consulted with the kids. Since Stephen's birthday fell on a Friday, I offered them the option of skipping school, but they preferred to stick to their normal routines, which included gymnastics for Zaia and baseball for Maddox. We decided to visit Stephen's grave and have a picnic two days later. We opted for a private gravesite visit, declining several offers or requests from other people to join us. Having others around, I believed, could potentially re-traumatize the kids by exposing them to intense emotions that were more for the adults' benefit. It could set them back emotionally to have people holding them tightly, crying, and pouring their grief onto them.

While I cried throughout the visit, the kids seemed fine. I asked them a few questions about their dad, but they weren't inclined to discuss him much. There was no cookie cake.

In November, Zaia turned four. No cookie cake for her either. We had a traditional layer cake, and nobody said a word. So maybe that's our new tradition.

What do you do to remember someone on the first anniversary of their self-inflicted death? We didn't know how, if at all, we should acknowledge the date of Stephen's suicide. I was going to be out of town on December 13. So the week before, we had a meal together in which we shared memories of Stephen. I knew the actual day was going to be a nightmare for me and for Weslie, the one child old enough to have the exact date burned in her mind. That morning, I FaceTimed with her. We both were brutally sad, but it helped to talk about how rotten we were feeling. Afterward, Weslie wrote an Instagram post about Stephen that made me a proud mama and melancholy in equal measure:

A year of missing you, but not a single day goes by without thinking of what you've given to the world. Your love, guidance, and wisdom continue to inspire me. Missing warm hugs, your wisdom, and the sound of your voice. Though the pain of your absence remains, I find serenity in the beautiful memories we shared. You were my father, my superhero, and my best friend, and my biggest advocate. Your love and support shaped me into the person I am today.

In retrospect, it probably was for the best that we weren't all together. I'm sure the littles would have been buffeted by my dark energy. I couldn't stop thinking that this is what our family's twelfth day before Christmas will look like forevermore.

For the holidays, I decorated multiple trees that we displayed in the house, but the personalized ornaments for the family tree remained packed away. The children helped me string the lights on the trees, but none of us was in any mood to unwrap all the memories that make our family ornament collection—a tradition I picked up from my mom—so cool. Anytime Stephen and I went anywhere with the children, to Hawaii for a weeklong vacation or to Disneyland for the day, we'd buy a trinket for the tree. Each one has a story behind it, and several of the baubles include family photographs. So, no, we couldn't go there in 2023.

It's up to me to figure out what our new Christmas tree tradition will look like. We've talked about starting a new ornament collection, and perhaps bringing back one of the old ones each year. Everyone can share a memory that it inspires before we hang it on the family tree alongside our new acquisitions. That's what it looks like to figure things out as we go.

Maddox and Zaia continue to attend school in Encino, which means that I'm back in the old neighborhood on a regular basis, using my own version of defensive maneuvers to avoid colliding with unwelcome memories. The routes I take no GPS would propose. I go out of my way to avoid driving past our old house on my way to drop off or collect Maddox.

Right after Stephen died, I worried that dancing would become something else to be avoided. If that ended up being the case, I'd have lost not only the love of my life but my first true love. I was initially paralyzed by my fear of dancing without him. If I didn't enjoy it the way I had before, it would be another crushing loss. However, as I delved into physical activities, including workouts and routines that connected me with my body, my anxiety ebbed.

Interestingly, music was never a trigger for me. Maybe it's because Stephen and I had danced to so many songs, everything from Frank Sinatra to Color Me Badd, that if I had to avoid everything that reminded me of him, the soundtrack of my life would become silence. The two exceptions are Adele's "One and Only," which was the first song we danced to at our wedding, and Jason Mraz's "I Won't Give Up," the song that played during our proposal. When I hear them, my mind instantly goes to Stephen, but not to the point where I break down in tears. Thank goodness for that. Otherwise, I'd be crying every day.

Music has the power to transport us back to indelible moments in our lives, and that's how it is for me. I'll hear a song to which Stephen and I danced on our backyard patio, which became our home stage, and it'll make me smile more often than it makes me sad. But dance is different. Dance had been a sacred language between us, so I had this crazy idea in my head that if I danced again, it would make Stephen's absence real.

As a result, rekindling my relationship with dance became a slow and cautious process. It took around seven months before I could muster the courage to put together a routine, and even then, the initial attempts were minimal—a tentative two-step. My dear friend Brittany Perry-Russell and I put together a fifteen-second routine to Missy Elliott's hit "Bomb Intro/ Pass That Dutch" shortly after the kids and I moved into the new house, and we posted our performance on social media. The dance teacher in me could see plenty to find fault with, technique-wise, but it felt so good to move my body like that again.

With Brittany's help, dancing became my personal love language. Before, I associated it with connecting with others, but now I see it as a means of reconnecting with myself. The dance was not only a tribute to my late husband, with whom I shared an unbreakable bond, but also a celebration of my individuality. And really, what is a marriage if not an intricate marathon dance, one in which you grow accustomed to relying on your partner for emotional support and companionship?

Now I was a soloist, with all the complex emotions that entailed: anger, sadness, and confusion, but also autonomy. The realization that even in solitude you can find moments of joy, connection, and love was a turning point for me. I must be honest, though; as a soloist, I am still gingerly finding my way. Eighteen months after losing Stephen, I have yet to dance a full routine, though I believe I'm getting close. When I am ready, I'm sure I'll invite some friends like Travis to help me through it.

I noticed that after I uploaded that dance with Brittany on Instagram, a few commenters expressed dismay, even disgust, at my decision to engage in a joyful activity so soon after Stephen's death. Moving forward at my own pace, choosing to attend concerts or walk red carpets, has drawn some harsh opinions on social media. People have a lot of opinions that they don't hesitate to share about how I should be handling my grief. My therapist encouraged me to imagine that I'm a mirror that people are seeing themselves reflected in so that I'm not beaten down by their opinions and feelings.

As with every other facet of my life, social media looks a little different to me in the wake of Stephen's death. It's been interesting for me to observe how differently I'm perceived by many people on social media now that Stephen is quite literally out of the picture. I'm posting the same kinds of photos now that I did when he was alive—on red carpets, dancing in the aisles of a sporting event, at the beach. When Stephen was by my side, we were celebrated. The comments were overwhelmingly positive and filled with love.

Now that he's gone, those same photographs rub some people the wrong way. They chastise me for calling attention to myself at a basketball game with my aisle moves—never mind that I'm standing behind my kid and literally pointing down at him to direct attention his way. It's as if I lost a husband and gained a group of social etiquette police. Literally the only thing different about my posts, then versus now, is Stephen was in them and now he's not.

I'm not Pollyanna. I know social media can foment hate and polarization. I feel sorry for the mean-spirited commenters. I really do. They deserve our empathy, not our enmity. I'm a firm believer that the meanest people on social media are projecting their own pain onto their targets. Instead of taking to heart their feedback, my heart goes out to them. What insecurities must they be harboring to lash out so virulently at someone they don't even know? Everyone is struggling with something, and when I see a mother of four, for example, taking apart in a social media post the outfit I chose to wear to a basketball game and my imprudence in dancing in the aisle during a TV time-out, well, it just makes me want to give her a hug.

I choose to focus on the army of people who have my back, those who have followed my journey and have supported me throughout, who are so resolute in their regard for me that they let the haters know not to come for me. Every single day, complete strangers defend me. They've supported me against those who have suggested I was somehow to blame for Stephen's death or that, at a minimum, I was a bad wife to have been so blindsided by it.

There are those who have expressed skepticism that someone so in love with his wife and children would take his own life and who have insinuated that there's more to the story. A few of the haters might have even been people close to Stephen. What does it say about our society that people are so comfortable tearing other people down? I'll never understand the psychology behind the vitriol. Are those few moments of satisfaction derived from brutalizing a stranger worth it? Why do we say these awful things to people if we're just saying them to be awful? Did no one's mother other than mine preach "Kill them with kindness"?

I'm eternally grateful for the people who will immediately come to my defense against those who try to destroy me. And the perfect strangers who will randomly reach out to ask, "How are you?" or say, "I hope your kids are doing okay."

Weslie has yearned to defend me against the trolls trafficking in dishonesty and deception, but I'm constantly reminding her of the power of silence. Engaging with them only gives their lies and hurtful comments more oxygen. "Let karma address those who attempt to harm us," I tell her. We strive to practice what amounts to a social media version of the Serenity Prayer: *God, grant me the self-restraint to ignore the hatred that we cannot change, the courage to speak out to support change in ourselves and others, and the wisdom to know the difference.*

If fame were a dance, it would be hardcore, with its driving rhythms and powerful drops and mix of electronic influences. It can be overwhelming at times to have everything in your life scrutinized, from your eyebrows to your relationships to your parenting style to your toddler's meltdown mid-meal at a restaurant. I've been told my boobs are too small and my stomach is too big and my legs are too short. From the time Stephen and I started dating, we received loads of hate based on our different skin colors. On the internet, people feel emboldened by the veil of anonymity or groupthink to deride us for being an interracial couple and then for creating a blended family. As if it's anybody's business but ours.

But you have to take the ugly with the beautiful, and Stephen and I had decided early on in our relationship that as long as we remained true to ourselves, we could handle the criticism. We adopted the philosophy that what other people say about us is none of our business.

It became a bit trickier as Weslie got old enough to engage with social media. I initially told her to steer clear of all comments under her posts. The mama bear in me wanted to shield her from prejudice and pettiness. But I gradually came to realize that there's no escaping the comments even when you're a confident adult. So I changed my approach. I told her to face the comments head-on while remembering you can't please everybody so you might as well be true to yourself.

I was super proud of preteen Weslie when she responded to a commenter on her TikTok page who asked her why she "dresses like a boy." In her video post, Weslie, who was twelve at the time, said, "Just because I don't wear dresses and bright pink doesn't mean I'm dressing like a boy."

She added, "This is my style. I wear comfy clothes and darker colors and just because I dress like that doesn't mean I'm dressing like a boy and it doesn't mean that boys or girls are defined by certain things because of their gender."

"It doesn't mean anything," she concluded, "and just because you can't open your eyes doesn't mean I'm about to change."

When I read her post, I knew I was doing a good job as a mom. Weslie is so wise and has seen so much, fortunately and unfortunately. She has seen my lifestyle. She has seen her father's lifestyle. She saw Stephen's lifestyle. She has experienced my lows with me. She has experienced my highs with me. She has experienced her father's highs and lows and Stephen's highs and lows. Somehow, throughout it all, she has held herself together so freaking well. It's beautiful to see how she has been able to choose a healthy path through the chaos, learning from the darkness but not succumbing to it.

The abrupt shift from a married life to involuntary singlehood was a disorienting experience. It made me question my identity and role in the world. Being a widow navigating parenthood alone adds another layer of complexity to my circumstances. In my mid-thirties, when I thought I was settling into one life, I was deposited, as if by a tornado, into a totally unfamiliar one. You don't experience the sudden loss of a spouse and come out the same person.

Some people find that very confusing. They don't want to see you evolve. They don't want you to change. Or maybe it's that they don't see you at all. People would call me and spend an hour or more unpacking their grief over Stephen's death, getting off their chests whatever they needed to get off their chests while I listened. I got several of these calls every day. In the beginning, I did my best to carry everyone's stories about Stephen. I drained myself trying. I didn't have the capacity to hold all their grief and mine. My kids and I appreciate people's support, but we can't be their healers when we are still healing ourselves.

Psychologist Susan Silk developed something called *ring theory*, which made a ton of sense to me. The premise is that in a crisis there exists a series of social rings. Those in the rings closest to the center—the person or people at the heart of the crisis—can unload their feelings, frustrations, and sorrows to those in the outer rings, who should refrain from offering anything other than comfort and compassion to those closer to the grieving core.

Listening to people talk at great length about how much they miss Stephen, I experienced moments of being traumatized over and over again. No one besides my family and my team had any patience for the fact that I was dealing with so much. I lost a lot of what I'd describe as casual friends, people who made it all about their trauma every time we talked. They cast themselves as the main character, not realizing it's not always their story. Stephen might have been amazing to them for one minute, but he was my everything for *every* minute—and he decided to leave and have no more minutes with me and the kids.

The new house was a huge step toward reclaiming the narrative that I felt had been hijacked from me. But now it has its own beloved resident ghost. My longtime and much-loved friend T.J., who was there for me in my hour of need, who truly saved me by coaxing me out of Encino, passed away eight months after the move. One of the first gatherings I hosted at the place he correctly identified as perfect for me was a repast with roughly one hundred guests in attendance.

I'd known that he had cancer. I'd accompanied him to some of his treatments. What he hadn't told me was that he was also battling a blood disease. He didn't want me to worry. He figured I was dealing with enough already, which pains me because I cared so much for him I would have gladly shared his burden. I text his husband regularly to check on how he's doing. Talking to him over the phone is trickier. How do I sit with and validate his grief over the loss of his partner without triggering my own? T.J.'s death was the blow that broke my fragile equanimity. In the days afterward, I was overcome by exhaustion, both emotional and physical.

I kept moving forward despite feeling overextended and over-whelmed. I was telling people I was taking on too much, but I wasn't doing anything to address it. I continued to rashly say yes to every business opportunity that came my way because I was determined to show people that Stephen's death had not broken me. I wanted people to see that I was handling by myself all the responsibilities that we had shared, without so much as missing a beat.

Four days after the celebration of T.J.'s life at my house, I crashed. I was surrounded by such beauty, but I couldn't see it because I was a hot mess. I canceled a video shoot at the last minute, with apologies to everyone involved, packed an overnight bag, and took off for a two-night stay at a technology-free retreat. I was proud of myself for recognizing, however belatedly, that in taking on so much for others I had lost the connection to myself. I needed to put on my oxygen mask first before helping those around me.

Weeks later, I booked a last-minute vacation to Monaco. I went by myself for five days. It was the first solo trip I could remember taking in a long time. I fed my soul with bicycle rides along the coast and a boat ride in the crystalline Mediterranean Sea and nourished my mind with books and fed my hunger with delicious meals. I posted a photograph of my bikini-clad self on social media and didn't worry my pretty little head when some commenters derided me for daring to look . . . happy.

While I may upset some, I'd like to believe that I'm helping others to realize that grief is not an excuse to withdraw from living. I had been existing for so long in survival mode, I wasn't able to access my creative side, which is what makes me me. I couldn't live in a constant state of mourning because then I'd be lost in a very dark place. That's not where I choose to be. That's where Stephen got stuck, and it was a treacherous space.

If I let his death keep me from living, then two of us will have died in that motel room.

Finding a balance between honoring my sadness and satisfying the very human need for moments of happiness and love is an ongoing and often confusing odyssey. I probably shouldn't have been surprised that the journey would carry me back to a familiar place.

CHAPTER 16

FINDING MY VOICE

I've always considered myself a storyteller, someone able to convey through my body the full range of human expression. Stephen used to say that he might not be a ridiculous wordsmith, but he was able to fearlessly express himself through dance. I felt the same way. I could tell profound truths without saying a word.

Throughout my career I had hidden behind my role as a dancer, focusing on the stories of others. After Stephen's suicide, our family's trauma drew considerable interest from news outlets. The prospect of telling my own story of love and loss was terrifying.

I expressed these fears in a conversation with my pastor. I said I felt I was being called upon to use my voice, but I wasn't sure how to discuss in public such a deeply personal tragedy. Stephen's death is such a sensitive subject involving someone I loved so much and didn't wish to dishonor. I didn't want to risk speaking out and saying the wrong things. It requires years of training for people to become authorities on grief, but I'd become a so-called expert in the field overnight.

"Perhaps this is your new purpose," he suggested. "Follow your intuition. When you let go of your control and speak from the heart, your words will come pouring out."

I considered his advice. There is such a taboo around suicide that dates back centuries, an enduring belief that, for religious and moral reasons, it is one of the gravest sins a human being can commit. Such dogmatic thinking fails to consider that the act can be inextricably linked to mental disorders or traumas that override or short-circuit an individual's freedom of choice.

For those whose loved ones die by suicide, grief mixes with anger and guilt and sadness and confusion. It can be difficult to address because this belief persists that to talk about suicide openly is to normalize it, causing potentially more people to take their own lives. To me, that's like saying we can't talk to teenagers about birth control because it will encourage them to have sex.

Did I have the courage to lead this conversation? The more I thought about it, the surer I felt that perhaps my pastor was right and I had been called to be a voice for those reeling from unspeakable grief. For whatever reason, the universe and God had dropped this challenge at my feet, and I was compelled to accept it. It was as if everything I've experienced in my life was preparing me to occupy this space.

Who better than me to help anyone contemplating suicide to see that their action will have far-reaching ripple effects that will buffet the lives of their friends and loved ones for a long, long time? Will they make a different decision if they know that the end of their pain will be the beginning of the pain their loved ones will endure?

And I want to comfort the grieving. To those who have been—or will be—visited by the same tragedy as my family, I want to offer assurances that there is life, and so much beauty, after a loved one's death, even when it is by their own hand. My purpose is to convey that with my words and deeds, even if I sometimes feel weak and rattled. I am asked all the time, "How are you doing—for real?" People see me sitting for interview after interview talking about Stephen's death and they wonder how I can be so composed. The truth is, there have been multiple times I've been scared to talk about what has happened, and in those moments it's as if God speaks through me.

Every time I scroll through my news feed, I'm reminded that someone somewhere has experienced a terrible loss. Everyone is going through something. If I wallow in my grief when so many others are suffering, how selfish would that make me? No person's trauma is more acute, more deserving of attention and sympathy. If anything, I'm more fortunate than most. I am surrounded by people supporting me and rooting for our family. I'd be terribly shortsighted not to pay that support forward however I can.

Once I had made the decision to tell my story, my priority became finding an outlet where I'd feel safe and protected. Five months after Stephen's death, I chose to sit down with Hoda Kotb on *Today*. I was so grateful for the space she provided for me to be vulnerable and true to my own narrative.

In conversation as in dance, I'm looking to lead through love and joy. Interestingly, even before my pastor spoke up, the medium I consulted mentioned during my reading that my life was meant to take this turn, that my purpose is to be a leader in the grief space. Both men and women who have lost their spouses in circumstances similar to mine have shared with me sentiments like "I felt stuck for years, but seeing you move forward, I'm inspired to do the same" or "I just lost someone, and witnessing your progress gives me hope that I'll be okay."

I'm saddened to have heard from so many men who say they haven't been honest with their partners or their parents about how they're feeling because they're meant to be the leaders in their families. They've been conditioned from a young age to suppress their feelings, to ignore their emotional discomfort. They have not been encouraged to view vulnerability as a strength. But I'm also heartened. Admitting these thoughts is an important first step, I believe, toward changing this tired, potentially dangerous gendered stereotype.

In death Stephen has helped so many people become more honest with their feelings. It's ironic since he couldn't manage it himself. I'll never forget a tribute the actor Tyler Perry posted on his Instagram page. After noting that Stephen always seemed full of life, he said:

I want to take you back to a time in my life when I tried to commit suicide, a couple of times, because it was so dark I didn't think it would get any better. I had endured so much pain, so much abuse, sexual abuse, it was all so hard to just move through, that I thought the only way to make this better was to end my life. Had any of those attempts happened, I would've missed the best part of my life. . . . Sometimes the pain is a buy-in. . . . all that pain, all that hell, all that struggle, if I had given up, if I had stopped, I wouldn't have seen the better part of my life. I was buying into something, I was paying for something.

This notion of hanging on because better days are ahead is such a powerful message. It would be easy to crumble, and trust me, I've had days where I feel broken. I allow myself those moments, but that's not where I want to linger. Living from trauma keeps you in trauma. I have to move toward living from a healed place—while recognizing, and accepting, that I'll never be fully healed.

I was reeling from the emotions—mine and other people's—that the first anniversary of Stephen's suicide dredged up, when I fielded a phone call from my agent with exciting news. I had been offered an opportunity to return to *So You Think You Can Dance* for Season 18 as a judge. I felt overwhelming gratitude and excitement. The show's set is my other home. It's the place where I feel the most myself. *SYTYCD* is where I established myself long before I met Stephen and became one half of a dancing power couple.

It was an honor to be asked back. Stephen had held the exact same job during Seasons 15 and 17. In the summer of 2022, months before he killed himself, he had campaigned for me to join him at the judges' table. We had had so many conversations in that vein because Stephen, being Stephen, believed I was more deserving of being on the panel than him. I was more schooled in the technical aspects of dance, so I was happy to deliver him notes on the performances as a kind of unofficial study buddy. But he made a great judge because of the way he treated people and nurtured them.

The truth is, I hadn't minded standing on the sidelines. The seasons in which Stephen served as a judge had been a nice respite for me. I could enjoy being a spectator and fan and appreciate the show without being involved in its production.

The offer to return to the show was a win-win as far as I was concerned. I knew I could make a positive contribution to the season, and the experience would be a step in the right direction for me. My only reservation was about leaving the kids every week to fly to Atlanta, where the show was being filmed. Would they worry that I wasn't coming back? Maddox had already informed me that he got nervous every time he returned home from school and I wasn't there. After mulling it over, I decided that for the sake of my healing—and the children's—I needed to take the job.

Their abandonment fears were not unfounded, given the circumstances. But it was important that they learn to trust the people they love to leave them and come back. It was hard the first couple of weeks, but the kids were in good hands with Korinne, whom they love like a big sister or aunt. And I made sure to FaceTime with them often.

Having been a contestant and an All-Star, I wondered if it would be weird for me not to be the one dancing on stage. What would it be like to not feed off the energy of the bright lights and the boisterous audience? I always felt like my best self when I was on the stage. Like I was ready to take on the world. I would get so amped up. I lived for the moment when I heard the click track and the cameras started rolling.

Having been a choreographer, I wondered if I'd feel strange not knowing every step I was about to see. But moving into a new role was like the seasons changing. I'm in, what, the autumn of my dancing career now? Whatever it is, it's a gorgeous period.

My stint as a judge and cohost with Maks Chmerkovskiy helped me rediscover my love of dance in a new capacity. It infused me with a new energy, for which I'm grateful. It was a relief, frankly, to find out that I didn't mind at all not being on the stage.

As soon as I reported to the set in Atlanta, I recognized what a wonderful gift it was that this door opened to me when it did. I was precisely where I needed to be. For half my life, my DNA had been entwined with the show's. For that reason, it was a little jarring when the social media chorus online took aim at me, with many commenters suggesting that I had been asked to judge only because I was the late tWitch's trophy wife. Huh? Those viewpoints would have been hilarious if they weren't so insulting. By the time the show brought Stephen and me together, I was an award-winning dancer and choreographer. Stephen's profile skyrocketed once he became a regular on Ellen's show, but I pulled my weight in our partnership.

As I mentioned earlier, when we undertook projects together, we were paid equally, which is a rarity in Hollywood. So to return to the show where my career took off and see myself described as the insignificant spouse of a dead man was hilarious. That said, after having been one half of a couple for so long, it was affirming to find out during the filmed auditions that not everybody looked at me and saw Stephen.

Bless the contestants who gave me back my groove by stepping onto the stage, one by one, and saying things like "I am auditioning because of you" or "I learned dance from you." It was a revelation. To think that the beautiful and talented young artists standing before me had been impacted and inspired by *my* dancing—it was, just, wow! Those dancer testimonies were a transformative moment for me, allowing me to extend the same grace to myself that I did the contestants. How funny that it took my becoming a judge to stop judging myself so harshly.

In another particularly touching moment, a young woman approached me and described a letter I'd written to her long ago when she was my student at Joffrey Ballet School in New York City. She'd kept the letter and a rose I'd given her. Her gratitude was obvious as she expressed how I had changed her life during that week of instruction. The lasting impact of mentorship was driven home to me as I witnessed her exquisite performance on the stage.

The narratives continued to unfold, each dancer conveying their own tales of triumphs and tribulations. Another courageous girl, who had endured her own trauma, shared that my presence was the sole reason she felt comfortable stepping onto the stage. The connections forged through these stories reaffirmed to me that I can still shape lives through dance.

One unforgettable instance involved a young dancer whose idol was Stephen. She bared her heart to the judges, revealing that her father had passed away. After her emotionally charged solo, she turned to me and shared words that resonated deeply: "I'm really, really inspired by the way you held yourself with grace and the way that you're holding tWitch's legacy. Thank you for continuing to be alive for us."

I was overcome by emotion. My tears flowed freely as I received validation for the purpose that drives me to put myself out there, vulnerabilities and all. I am a firm believer that sometimes God or the universe recognizes when we need a gentle nudge of encouragement. During a period where my daily self-affirmations (*I love myself . . . I can do hard things*) had lost their resonance, divine intervention restored my focus to where it needed to be. Returning to the show was an immensely gratifying experience. It served as a testament to the good I have done in the dancing world.

I'm convinced that my return to the show was the universe's way of compelling me to reclaim my past—all of it—to help me shape a constructive future. The outpouring of support I received was overwhelming. It's ironic that the show saved me when I was eighteen and lost and living in Utah, again when I was a single mom and lost and living in LA, and once more when I was thirty-six and lost and living as a widow.

The only way any of it makes sense is to conclude that God is working through me. He surely has tested my faith. Good thing I know just where to go for spiritual guidance.

CHAPTER 17

MOVING FORWARD
STEP-BY-STEP

E veryone talks about how difficult the first year is after a spouse's death, and they're not wrong. But what doesn't get emphasized enough is that the second year is equally brutal. While I've navigated all the "firsts," I'm here to tell you that they aren't appreciably easier to negotiate the second time around. So many people told me that once I got through the first year without Stephen that I'd be fine, and in some areas, they were right. In many respects my family and I have healed.

We've grown more comfortable with Stephen being gone. As we moved deeper into 2024, we entered a new phase, one in which it was okay to bring him up in conversation without getting triggered. We could say "Remember when Dad did this?" and even if the memory did end up stirring up heavy feelings, we were able to talk it out. Just as significantly, we've grown more comfortable creating new traditions and memories that have nothing to do with Stephen.

At the same time, I'm confronted with situations that are a sobering reminder that I may not necessarily be through the worst of it. I used to hate the word *survivor* because it makes me think of *enduring*, and my focus has always been on *thriving*. But I've gradually gained a new appreciation for the act of simply enduring. Before I could flourish, I had to learn how to live my life from the healed version of who I am. Even if I wanted to formulate a five-year plan as I used to do as a matter of course, I was in my trauma silo, viewing my world through the lens of a survivor, not a thriver.

Survivor is a tricky word for me, but you know which word really gets caught in my throat? *Suicide*. It's not a noun—it's a stain. I spent the first year and a half talking around the word. I was so scared of saying out loud, "My husband died by suicide." It's such a sad word that conjures violence and finality. I had to learn to say *suicide* because, like it or not, it is now a part of my story. I still struggle with the word, but I have to learn to accept it—and say it.

Have you noticed that there is no word in the English vocabulary to denote someone left behind by someone who died by suicide? Suicide is so toxic a topic and so triggering for those impacted by it, we can't even assign a term to the true victims. Technically speaking, my kids and I are survivors of suicide. But if I say that, it sounds as if we are the ones who attempted to kill ourselves. Should I describe myself as *suicide adjacent*? An *intentional widow*?

Contrary to the belief that the loss of a spouse gets easier with time, it's more accurate to say it grows familiar. The pain and longing become wedged in your heart like impossible-to-extract splinters. This year will be characterized by another Valentine's Day without flowers from my husband. Another Father's Day spent sharing memories *of* Stephen instead of making more *with* him. Another September in which we don't perform our annual dance routine to Earth, Wind & Fire's "September" to mark Stephen's birth month. Another year of mornings without Stephen reversing my car out of the driveway because I was so freaked out after I backed into our fence post.

The daily grind is an intricate dance of two steps forward and one step back, of veering off course, of finding the strength to return to the path. Accepting that this is my lot in life now has been hard to swallow. I didn't deserve this. Yet here I am. All I can do is act with grace, stay true to who I am, and not lose sight of who I want to become.

I never wanted to come across as a bad wife or a bitter widow by pointing out what seems patently obvious: If Stephen had abandoned me and the kids by taking off without paying child support and never bothering to see his children again, his actions naturally would have come under unflattering scrutiny. People would have said, "How dare he not be there for his kids? I thought he was so great, but what a jerk!"

But because he left me and the kids by taking his life (such a sanitized way of putting it), the public discourse is altogether different. Perhaps it's because people don't know how to talk about suicide and are fearful of coming across as judgmental, but it seems as if Stephen has been romanticized in death, and that's messed up.

People gush about how he was such a good friend, such a great dad. So kind. So caring. I hear this stuff and I nod my head and think, *Yeah, you're right. He was all those things.* But if I'm honest, I'm also thinking to myself, rather uncharitably, *But he also destroyed our family leaving the way he did, and he had been keeping a lot of secrets.* The celebration of suicide, an inherently selfish act, at the expense of the living is a wrong that needs to be set right.

You risk looking like a real jerk if you call out somebody who took their own life. They're not around to defend themselves, and it's impossible to know what they were thinking. Stephen was a wonderful husband and father, *and* he crushed me and my children by leaving the way he did. Both things are true, but I don't think people want to hear that from me. I'm weary of hearing, "Oh, poor Stephen." What about poor Stephen's kids who have had to deal with the aftermath of his actions?

Because I've been a public figure since I was a teenager, people tend to forget that I'm a mother, I'm a sister, I'm a *human*. So while I miss Stephen and mourn the loss of my husband and best friend and business partner and dancing companion, I don't have any choice but to move forward. I can't look back. I can't afford to miss a step because I have to be there for the three little humans I love so much and who are now solely my responsibility.

It's not intentional, but I don't think people have given my kids enough grace through all this. They haven't been given the space to process that Stephen was a great father who abandoned them. At first, all the tributes—his inclusion in the 75th Emmys "In Memoriam" segment quickly comes to mind—were beautiful. To see Stephen's face right after Angela Lansbury's and directly before Richard Belzer's was amazing. Also awful, if I'm being honest. I was happy to see Stephen celebrated, but that didn't mean it didn't hurt me and the kids because it reminded us of what we'd lost.

One, almost two years on . . . the tributes hit a little differently. Anytime anyone says, "I loved your husband," I think, *Me too, but I'm also really, really angry at him for abandoning me.* I just wish fans could see him not just through their lenses but also through the lenses of the children he left behind, who will never again experience his awesomeness and who are still traumatized by how he left them.

Here's an example of the complexity of our situation—a complexity that too often goes unremarked upon. In 2024, Weslie turned sixteen. In my mind, this birthday was a marker of a childhood receding far too fast. I can't remember how I spent my sixteenth birthday. I'm not sure any photographs exist to jog my memory. I recall only that it fell on a Friday, which means I was likely on a plane headed out of town to work at a dance convention. I wanted this milestone birthday to be a grand occasion for her, and the original plan was to throw a blowout bash attended by a few dozen guests with no expense spared. I wanted Weslie to have an indelible memory of this day, joyful images that she could access for the rest of her life.

At first, she enthusiastically embraced the idea of the party. But as the date drew closer and the details were being finalized, she expressed a sudden change of heart. She spoke in vague terms about her unease. She was struggling with so many emotions. It didn't require an emergency session with my therapist to see what was going on.

My sense was that Weslie wanted to have an amazing party to prove to herself and her classmates that she was perfectly fine. In theory, the plans sounded terrific, but in practice, a Sweet 16 celebration minus Stephen was too much for her to process. Weslie was overwhelmed by the push and pull of love and bitterness, nostalgia and resentment—the same competing impulses that we've all been experiencing.

I felt as if I'd let her down big-time. In my desire to give her a happy memory and to nudge her closer to whatever our new normal looks like, I had failed to intuit that she wasn't okay. I should have been able to read her ambivalence. I could have done a better job of seeing her, of making room for the possibility that she was indulging my wishes to make me feel better—my little protector, to a fault.

I left the decision up to her. At the end of the day, she settled on a birthday cake with the family and a shopping trip to Beverly Hills's iconic Rodeo Drive with her best girlfriends. We ate at a tucked-away spot—it's not called The Hideaway for nothing—and the meal was filled with such laughter and lightness that I knew in my heart this birthday had unfolded precisely as it was meant to. But arriving at that point was a trial.

Stephen should have been leading everyone in singing "Happy Birthday" to Weslie. I have to constantly reassure my children that they are not the reason he decided not to stick around. I can no longer give Stephen a pass and say he was a hero. Because he was a human being. Period.

When I returned to the set of *So You Think You Can Dance* as a judge, one colleague I hadn't seen in several years immediately started reminiscing about Stephen and talking about their grief over his loss. Of course they did. They mourned his absence too. Still, the conversation rattled me. I didn't want to start crying and smear my makeup. I refrained from voicing my discomfort because I knew they meant well. It would be so helpful if people could be mindful of the purity of their memories and how mine are bound to be much more complex. Stephen wasn't taken away from us prematurely; he decided to leave us. That adds darkness to the kindness and light with which he is remembered.

In such conversations with grieving loved ones, be patient. Handle the topic, and the person to whom you're talking, gently. Let them lead the way and be content to follow.

We're all figuring out this wild ride called life as we go along. My responsibility is to show up every day with love and light. It's one thing to do that for my children, but to also do that for the millions of strangers who think they know you can be challenging. If I could offer one piece of advice for interacting with people in circumstances like mine, it would be to remember, when in doubt, to follow Silk's ring theory. Maybe it's because I was never an A- or B-list celebrity, but I've done my best over the years to meet everyone else where they are. Stephen was the same way. If people could afford me the same courtesy, I would be so grateful.

I do genuinely want people to feel they can open up to me. I want them to feel heard and understood. I want to be able to help them through whatever loss they're struggling with. But I can get knocked over by a wave of grief without warning, and when that happens, what do I do? If I succumb to my emotions, if I break down and can't be there for people the way they need me to be, will they see me as "less than"?

So many people depend on me to be their support system, and I'm scared that if I tell them that I'm not okay—or they can clearly see that I'm not okay—they won't lean on me anymore. And I want to be there for them. I don't want them to see me as weak. I struggle with not wanting to expose my vulnerability. I want to be a light for people. I don't want people to run at the sight of me because I'm a downer.

My therapist has suggested that my not asking for help is a defense mechanism, my way of protecting myself from being rejected by people whose respect I want. Somewhere along the way, I got it into my head that I can't admit to feeling scared, embarrassed, or stupid because if people saw me that way, they wouldn't love me. I don't know how to uncross that wiring.

And yet, if I deny my feelings, I'm repeating Stephen's mistake.

Father's Day is a real trigger for the kids and me. It has a way of ambushing us. In the lead-up to the third Sunday in June, we are inundated with commercials and conversations that revolve around a dad's bond with his kids or gifts that Dad will love. There's no escaping it, and it's a lot to handle. As our second Father's Day without Stephen drew closer, I observed my children cycling through anger, sadness, and resentment as if binge-feeling emotions.

I wanted to turn the occasion into something positive for them. I wasn't convinced that sharing memories about Stephen while eating a picnic lunch at the cemetery, like we did in 2023, was the best choice. I'm still struggling to find a balance between their immediate comfort and the recognition that there's no escaping this holiday. It's going to come around every year whether we like it or not. All we can do is face it. We're talking about a lifetime of Father's Days that they'll have to soldier through. It's my job to arm them with the tools that will make them the strongest individuals you'll ever meet so that a lifetime of Father's Days doesn't break them.

The Sunday before Father's Day 2024, the lead pastor at Mosaic, who's a dear friend, delivered a powerful lesson that seemed directed at me. It was about helping people and allowing yourself to be helped, about letting the love you send into the world shore you up instead of wear you out. As he was speaking, I was reminded of Stephen, who took all the love he received and gave it away to others instead of holding on to some of it for himself. It occurred to me that I had been doing the same thing, giving away so much of myself that I had nothing left for me. That was why I had been feeling totally drained.

I've never felt comfortable asking people for help. Since Stephen's death, I've asked so much of the people I love the most—too much, especially considering I know that Stephen's death still weighs heavily on all of them. I don't know how to get past that. It makes me mad at Stephen for making me depend so much on other people because I no longer can depend on him. I see how people have to be so much for me, and it hurts.

I thought I was doing a good job of internalizing that pain. I thought so even after the pastor and his wife invited me to lunch a few days later. Once we were seated, they asked how I was doing. I supplied my usual answer. "We're *fine!* Me and the kids are doing *great!*" They let me rattle on for fifteen minutes about how well things were going. They sat quietly as I ran through my whole spiel.

And then the pastor said, "Okay, are you ready now to actually talk? Are you ready for a real conversation?"

Oh. My. Gosh. I've never felt so called out in my entire life. I was like, *What just happened? I didn't give you guys anything.* Feigning ignorance, I said, "What do you mean?"

He replied, "We know you. We care about you. Tell us what you're going through. Are you really okay? It seems to us as if you're keeping yourself busy so you don't have time to sit with your feelings."

Busted. But my pastor wasn't finished. "When are you going to stop acting like Stephen's the hero?" he said. He could have knocked me over with a feather, I was so taken aback. "You know we love you," he said. "You know we loved Stephen. But we've been watching you all year continue to put yourself in the line of fire and praise him. I love all the interviews you've been doing. I've watched every one of them. I love the spirit you have. But you cannot promote Stephen as the hero anymore. It's okay to talk about how he made the wrong choice."

I'll never, ever forget what he said next: "Allison, you and your kids are the heroes here. If no one's told you that, I want to be the first to say it. You're the ones left behind to pick up the pieces."

I was grateful for that point of view. It was hard to hear because I want so much to celebrate Stephen's memory, but I understood what he was driving at. To celebrate Stephen is to risk giving someone a pass to make the same choice that will plunge their family members into the same hell.

I was more than Stephen's wife. I'm the mother of his children, and it's hard for me to see what they've been put through. I sometimes talk so softly about their circumstances because I don't want to make them feel any worse than they already do. But for anyone contemplating an exit like Stephen's, I want them to realize the gravity of their decision on the people they would leave behind.

Weslie had asked Stephen if he would walk her down the aisle when or if she got married, and now that will never happen. If she does have a wedding—and hopefully she'll only have one—that memory will be a stain. Maddox will never have Stephen in the stands at one of his basketball games. He will never say to Stephen, "Dad, I want you to meet my first girlfriend." Zaia will never get to experience Stephen walking her to her first day of school. There's nothing I can say or do to diminish their pain, and that is hard to accept.

While I understood my pastor's point about Stephen, I still felt reluctant to acknowledge my own role. "You'll have to forgive me," I said, "if most of the time I don't feel like a hero."

He said that it's okay for me to acknowledge that I'm still going through hard stuff. I was candid. I admitted that it's difficult to speak openly about what the kids and I have been through. I don't know how to talk about his legacy. Unfortunately, I don't relate at all to what Stephen did, and that makes me sad. It's like, *What were you thinking?*

I had a strong sense during my session with the medium that he's at peace, which is confusing because I don't want anyone to think his choice was okay. Whatever he was dealing with, this was the only way he saw to keep us safe. I don't need my kids to accept his decision to kill himself. But I choose to have empathy for him because it will help their healing.

For myself, I choose life and the lives of my kids. If we devote the rest of our lives to honoring him, then we're existing from a place of sorrow, not joy. If people want to hold on to an image of me with him, that's fine, but *I* can't do it anymore. I'm not the same person who was Stephen's wife, and I must own that. I'm a new human, and I'm not scared to say so. Stepping into a new power won't diminish my love for Stephen or his legacy. I can no longer devote all my energy to absorbing people's pain over what Stephen did, covering up my own pain in the process. I'm giving myself permission to evolve instead of waiting for someone to come along and choreograph the rest of my life—or worse, allow Stephen, in his absence, to set the parameters and establish the story.

The kids and I ended up spending our second Father's Day without

Stephen at the Fairfax flea market. In honor of him, we wore matching Air Jordan sneakers. As we wove our way around the booths, we shared our favorite stories about him. Joyful stories. Stories that made us laugh out loud.

I gave each kid a twenty-dollar bill and challenged them to use it to sniff out the best bargain. Four-year-old Zaia was the runaway winner. She struck a hard bargain with a local artisan, walking away with a twenty-dollar necklace inspired by Leonardo da Vinci's *Vitruvian Man* for one dollar. Her face lit up like a lantern when the woman gave her the piece of jewelry. I rushed in right behind my baby bargain bandit and offered to pay the artist the difference between what the necklace was worth and what Zaia had paid for it, but she refused to take my money. The delight on Zaia's face when she handed her the necklace was easily worth nineteen dollars, she said.

We ended up at the flea market because we had attended Weslie's boyfriend's basketball game nearby. Maddox, a hoops fanatic, wouldn't have missed the game for the world. He has become the team's unofficial mascot. Weslie's boyfriend lets Maddox tag along with him to shootarounds, and he and his teammates, bless their freaking hearts, have him retrieve rebounds and encourage him to take the occasional shot. Maddox couldn't be happier if he were fetching loose balls for LeBron James. (Steph Curry is another story. Maddox loves Steph more than basketball itself.)

Maddox is playing basketball on a summer travel team and has drawn praise from his coach for his playing acumen. To be surrounded by all this male energy is exactly what he needs right now. Basketball, a trip to the barber shop (which was a great success, by the way)—I'm doing all I can to surround Maddox with men, including Black men, to fill the immense void Stephen left.

The flea market and the basketball game were so much fun, and as we tucked into delicious Italian fare at Jon and Vinny's, everyone agreed that it had been a Father's Day well spent. The love we have for Stephen, and the love he showered on us, is not gone. We could feel his presence on Father's Day, as we feel it every day. My kids talk about how his love lingers with us. The challenge is to keep alive his memory without being dragged down by it.

A year and a half after Stephen's death, there are moments when his absence still feels so raw. I was reminded that any of us can come unglued, triggered by the most innocuous circumstances, during a Fourth of July trip to visit my family in Utah. The kids love being around all their cousins. One day my brother Dave and his three small boys accompanied me, Maddox, and Zaia on a four-mile hike along the Big Springs Hollow Loop in Provo, an ambitious task for five kids under the age of ten. The scenery was gorgeous—really grounding. Along the way Dave, who is a fantastic dad, served as tour guide, pointing out animal tracks and dispensing commonsense survival tips, like following a body of water downstream if you get lost.

The more fatigued Zaia became, the more she complained to me. Maddox came to my defense, upbraiding his sister for picking on me.

"It's all right," I said to him. "You don't need to be my protector."

When we stopped to eat the snacks we had packed, Maddox abruptly burst into tears and ran away from the group. I recognized that cry. It was so gut-wrenching that it could mean only one thing: Whatever was troubling him, it involved his dad.

I chased after Maddox. When I caught up to him, he collapsed in my arms. I held him tightly and rocked him until his weeping gradually tapered off.

At first, Maddox wouldn't tell me what was wrong. "That's okay," I said. "I'll sit here with you until you feel comfortable talking."

We sat in companionable silence for a while, and then Maddox abruptly unleashed a primal scream: "*I wish Daddy was here!*" Obviously, seeing his cousins interact with their dad had set him off.

It's inevitable that he's going to come across fathers and sons doing father-and-son things. My job is to equip him with coping techniques. In this case, I validated his pain. "I wish Daddy was here, too, baby. It's okay to feel that way. I feel that way all the time." I added, "But I also feel like

Dad is watching us all the time. Do you feel that way? Do you feel Daddy in your heart?"

He nodded. We did some calming breathwork and I reassured him that I'm not going anywhere.

"I've got you, baby," I said. "I'm here."

Like a pop-up storm, Maddox's emotional outburst ran its course. When we returned to the group, Zaia gave Maddox a big hug. We resumed walking, and Maddox skipped ahead with his two older cousins, back to being his lighthearted self. I could hear Maddox sharing memories about Stephen, telling his cousins how his daddy used to throw him in the air and catch him and toss him on the bed. Pretty soon they all were laughing.

Be calm, my beating heart. Over time, that's the biggest change I've noticed in my kids: their ability to ride out their lows without getting stuck or consumed by them. What used to level them for a day or more now can be defused in a matter of minutes. They are able to release their big, bold emotions instead of stuffing them down. They know they'll be listened to, and when they're through, we'll hug it out.

The hike took an unexpected turn when my brother's six-year-old, Calvin, let the other boys go ahead and held back to wait for me. Their conversation about dads had gotten him thinking. "Shouldn't Maddox have a stepdad now that his dad isn't here anymore?" he said solemnly.

Zaia perked up. "Do I get a new dad?" she asked. "That could be fun!"

From the mouths of babes. I'm still uncovering new insights about myself, my relationships with my kids, my history with Stephen. Could I love someone again? Could I *be loved* by someone else? As hard as it is for me to imagine, I want to keep myself open to the possibilities.

To make space in my life for whatever the fates will allow, I first had to rethink my definition of *alone* and reconsider how I perceived the word. I'm ashamed to say that I haven't always acknowledged the support that's right in front of my nose. I spent so much time sitting across from friends, saying how I felt so alone. They were so sweet and so supportive, these people who would literally do anything for me. Looking back, it's like, *Allison, a little self-awareness, please.* Here I was, with amazing kids, a supportive family, friends and coworkers and team members who would do anything for me, and I had the nerve to talk about how *alone* I was feeling?

I think of Andy Grammer, my onetime *Dancing with the Stars* partner, who was one of the first people to reach out to me after Stephen's passing. (How neat is that?) We had done a dance to honor his deceased mother, and when he called me after hearing about Stephen, he made me laugh and he made it safe for me to give voice to how scared I was. He assured me that I was going to be okay.

And how could I possibly say I was alone when I have a friend like Travis, who came over after Stephen died, disappeared into my closet, and emerged wearing my fur jacket, then a series of jaunty hats, followed by a dress or two in the most hilarious drag show ever? His actions transported me back to our teenage years on the *So You Think You Can Dance* tour. It was the silly interlude that I needed. Not for nothing, he was also the one who pointed to my Prada suit, the gift from Stephen that was still wrapped in its box, and said, "A black suit, Allison? Really?" That suit, incidentally, remains in its box, never worn, tucked away in the storage unit.

While I'm at it, I'd like to give a shout-out, and an apology, to a special group of people. Only recently has it dawned on me that I let the actions of a few mean girls at the dance studio in Orem unfairly cloud my childhood memories. It wasn't until after Stephen died that I realized how uncharitable I'd been to the dancers—and there were many—who had unfailingly shown up for me. This epiphany came on the day I received in the mail Minky Couture blankets for me, Weslie, Maddox, and Zaia from members of my premier dance team, who had held a fundraiser to buy the gifts, which came with handwritten cards for each of us. I was filled with gratitude for how willing they were to be there for me, even from a distance. Those blankets we wrapped around us were the closest things to hugs that could be sent through the mail.

There were so many lovely gestures that took me a while to unpack but that I want people to know have not gone unnoticed. I feel terrible that I pushed away people who were nothing but supportive. There was so much beauty all around me, and I'm ashamed that I let negativity and confusion keep me from seeing it.

It made me think of Stephen. Did he have any idea how loved he was? If he knew how many people he grew up with and around in Alabama cared so much for him and were so supportive, maybe he'd still be here. If you know that one person sees you and loves you, shouldn't that be enough to endure anything?

When you lose a spouse, the pain is so intense, it feels as if you've lost a part of yourself. In that context, I defined *alone* as being without a life partner. I had to figure out for myself that the void left by Stephen's death could be filled by other people who already loved me. I didn't need a new love to feel whole. I just needed to lean into my friends—all of them, wherever they were. I could give them more of a role in my day-to-day life and communicate what I needed from them, which I'd never done: Would you dance with me the way I used to dance with Stephen? Could I bounce business ideas off you the way I used to seek Stephen's counsel?

I would do it all again, you know, which is wild to admit. I loved Stephen so much that I would do it all over again, even knowing how it would end. Until recently, I wasn't sure I deserved another great relationship. But as I've done the work to heal, I've had a shift in perspective. What if it wasn't luck that enabled me to have thirteen years of a grand love with Stephen? What if I attract that kind of love? It's a lovely thought, anyway, to consider that I might be able to find it again.

It was fitting that my nephew should choose the hike to ask his question. There's nothing like being surrounded by the splendor of nature to call to mind the changing seasons. Whether by choice or not, we're constantly going to be thrust into these new phases and chapters. Will the kids ever get a new dad? Who knows what the future will bring.

"We'll just have to wait and see," I said.

I had forgotten the beauty of my home state. A scenic drive around the twenty-mile Alpine Loop gave me a schooling in resilience. Everywhere

I looked in the canyons of the Wasatch Range were trees that have had to adapt to survive harsh conditions. They've had to fight for sunlight, for water, and they wear the scars of the battles they've waged. They're permanently bent by the wind or missing branches. There's beauty in their brokenness. No one sees a tree and says, "Ugh, look at all those missing branches. What a pathetic conifer." I needed the reminder that what matters in life isn't perfect symmetry but staying grounded and weathering all manner of storms.

I don't talk to Stephen anymore like I did the first year he was gone, and that's okay. I no longer feel tethered to him. The kids and I are slowly but surely shaking free of the trauma that chained us to him. I don't doubt that Stephen is watching over us, and that gives me comfort. But I no longer rely on him the way I used to. I trust my own instincts a lot more. A year ago, I couldn't have seen a way forward that gave me a clear view of the horizon.

CHAPTER 18

NEW ROUTINES

My decade-long morning routine died with Stephen. No longer must I stay upstairs until seven so my husband can have his hour of uninterrupted peace. Now I'm the one who wakes up every day at six, pads downstairs, and makes coffee for myself. I bought a fancy machine and thoroughly enjoy the process of grinding Stumptown beans in it, frothing oat milk or almond milk, and making myself a scalding-hot vanilla latte using bottled syrup. I don't drink out of the Superman mug that Stephen unfailingly used for my coffee. Like so many other items that carry memories of him, that mug is tucked away in a box in our storage unit.

Once I have my coffee in hand, I slip outside to the backyard and lower myself into my ice-cold bath, which is set at fifty degrees. I immerse myself, gasping as I go, until my body is numb from the neck down. In those frozen three to five minutes, I achieve a state close to nirvana—a profound peace of mind that I can only achieve otherwise through dance. Cold plunging has become my daily go-to activity for reasons that go well beyond the physical jolt. It's like hitting the reset button. My circulation startles to life, waking my body from the inside out. Endorphins flood my system, giving me a natural high. It's a meditative exercise that leaves me in a Zen-like state.

I believe in it so much that I've gotten my kids to try it. I'm not going to lie. You have to get through the first few weeks. It's painful at first, but I've learned to crave the pain. I really do look forward to it each morning. If I don't get in my cold plunge, for whatever reason, my body and mind don't feel quite right.

I can work on my core strength and meticulously maintain my physical appearance, but I'm not going to reap the full benefits of my efforts in either area if my head isn't in the game. Now more than ever, I value and prioritize my mental well-being. I ask for help, however awkward I feel doing so, when I need it. I wish I could have impressed upon Stephen to do the same.

I'll spend a few minutes every morning at my vanity, tending to my hair and makeup while showering myself in affirmations. *I'm smart. I'm kind. I can do hard things. I love myself.* I'm a fervent believer in manifestations and affirmations, so much so that I kicked off 2024 by having each family member choose three words to serve as a guide for the new year. Mine were *intention*, *forward*, and *discipline*—words that keep me on track to positively impact those who are facing challenges of their own.

I included *discipline* because it's the foundation from which so much else sprouts, including self-confidence and self-worth. Our affirmations are more than a morning exercise; they're a deliberate choice to shape the way we perceive ourselves and the world around us. The power of our internal dialogue is profound. We talk to ourselves more than anyone else does. Those self-directed words carry a weight that transcends external influences. They become the narrative that defines our self-worth and forms our perspectives.

My time in front of my vanity is not about getting all glammed up. Truth be told, most days I'm wearing sweats. The affirmations root me to the moment, which makes it easier for me to present the best version of myself to the world. Feeling good about myself is the real goal here. When I've got that makeup on, I'm not just putting my face together. I'm putting my best self forward.

My "me time" is the furthest thing from an ego exercise. It's about setting the tone for a day of energy and purpose. Without it, I wouldn't have survived the past year and a half. I'd be here in a physical sense, don't get me wrong. But I wouldn't have made the same spiritual strides. And I don't believe my children would be coping as well as they appear to be.

In recent weeks I've noticed that I wake up every morning and it feels normal that Stephen is not here. I'm not reaching out and patting his side of the bed, expecting to find him. I don't wake up looking forward to our first morning kiss. I'm no longer tripped up by his absence. I don't wake up asking myself why he decided to leave us. The other day, I awakened feeling *gleeful*. Some people in my position are scared to say that, as if they are somehow betraying the dead for feeling happy or content.

I am love. I have love. I deserve love.

With my affirmations and makeup done, I'll wake up Maddox and Zaia, if they aren't already up, and help Zaia get dressed for school. I'll wake up Weslie if she has slept through her 6:30 alarm, which she does without fail. I'll help Korinne, who usually arrives around this time, fix breakfast and pack lunches. I'll make one of the school runs with either Weslie or the littles, and if I'm in the car with Maddox and Zaia, I will make sure they repeat their daily affirmations. I'll start the sentence and let them finish: *I am . . . strong. I am . . . smart. I am . . . kind. I am . . . beautiful. I can do . . . hard things.*

Maddox being Maddox, he'll add, *I am . . . handsome.*

I encourage them to recite these phrases like a mantra whenever they face challenges or feel as if they're headed toward a meltdown. The idea is to reinforce a positive mindset even in the face of hard things. How else are my kids going to develop resilience, confidence, and self-esteem? It's funny—even when I'm in the driver's seat, I don't always know where I'm going, and yet my kids are counting on me to show them the way.

After the school run, I'll meet with a trainer for a solid workout or otherwise carve out time for some physical activity, even if it's just a brisk walk. And then my workday begins: phone calls and Zoom meetings and interviews and shoots. I'm generally busy until it's time to pick up the littles from school. Once back at home, I'll fix them a snack and prepare dinner. After we finish eating as a family, we'll take a dip in the jacuzzi and sometimes play cards or a board game.

As in most households with small children, we have bedtime routines aimed at increasing our littles' sense of security and teaching them how to fall asleep on their own. Zaia is the first to go to bed, and every night after I take her to her room, Maddox will stick his head in and say, "Hey, is everything good?" He wants to make sure that Zaia is okay—he is *very* protective of his little sister—but he also doesn't want me to forget about him. I tell him I'll finish reading Zaia a story and then I'll be in to tuck him in and say goodnight.

I didn't know this until Weslie told me, but after I put Maddox to bed one night, he didn't stay there. He tiptoed into her room, which is next to his, and asked her if she could turn her TV back on. Weslie told him that she had turned it off because she was going to sleep.

"I know," he said, "but can you turn it back on so I can sleep?"

He told her that when he didn't hear her TV, he had to check on her to make sure she was okay. He is able to rest easier with her TV on because the sound offers him assurances that she is there. Since then, Weslie has slept every night with her TV on, which is sweet but also sad.

It's beautiful that Weslie looks after her little brother. She doesn't do it because I've asked her to but out of pure love for him. And I'm proud that Maddox feels safe to be vulnerable and open up to her like that. But I wish he didn't have a reason to be anxious that he could be abandoned suddenly by someone to whom he is so deeply attached.

We've always been a tight-knit family, but after what we've gone through my kids have grown even closer. They're best friends. They lean on one another so much. They've got one another's backs. It is healing for me to experience as a parent the inseparable family unit that I have as an adult and longed for as a child.

Weslie will bring her school friends home to play with Maddox and Zaia. If it's a movie night, Maddox and Zaia will rummage around in the pantry for snacks, which they'll arrange on a tray and serve to Weslie and her friends.

Weslie has always been protective of me, but since Stephen's death, she has been hypervigilant. She needs to know where I am 24/7 or else she worries. She downloaded an app on my phone that tracks family members and their locations. She is constantly checking on me. If I'm unreachable, it is very triggering for her.

One day in the spring of 2024 I went out to lunch with a girlfriend. I received a text from Weslie: "Where are you?" When I didn't respond, she texted me again: "Where are you?" I didn't see either of her messages. My phone had stayed in my purse because I wanted to focus on my friend and our conversation.

Back at home, Weslie and her boyfriend sailed through the front door after school and swept into the kitchen where I was preparing afternoon snacks. They started interrogating me. "What were you doing today?"

I told them about the lunch with my friend. I casually mentioned that I ran into another friend, Terrell, at a grocery store in the same strip mall as the restaurant.

Weslie's voice rose. "You didn't tell me you were going out for lunch today," she said.

I replied that I was unaware that I had to keep my child abreast of my schedule. What did she think, I added, that I stayed home all day waiting for her to return?

"Yes!" she said. "I just find it really interesting, Mother, that you were out all day. You were at lunch and I didn't know. And I saw you hug a guy!"

Wait. What? She saw me hug Terrell? How was that possible? Now I became the interrogator. "You mean my friend who I ran into at the grocery store who embraced me out of sympathy because of what we went through?" I said. How on earth did she know about him?

Weslie and her boyfriend exchanged looks. They shifted their weight uncomfortably from one leg to the other. They'd been so worried, Weslie explained, that they ditched school, tracked me to the restaurant on the location app, and sat in the parking lot spying on me. I didn't know whether to laugh or cry. It's a harmless story, almost humorous, but painful and upsetting too.

We engage in open dialogue and hard conversations that have opened my eyes to how much they pick up on and understand. I never want them to hold back from asking me anything, no matter how uncomfortable it might make them—or me. Our resilience is hard-won. The past is the past. We can't go back. All we can do is keep moving forward. Our focus is on what's next. Every day we ask, "Who do we want to become?" and then set about inching in that direction.

The wisdom that every season has its expiration date has been helpful in guiding me through the highs and lows. *This too shall pass.* Times of joy or heartbreak—both are transient. This mindset anchors me when grief is threatening to knock me down. The pain, I tell myself, will eventually run its course. The ephemeral nature of life has nudged me to savor its richness, to breathe in the sky, the trees, the stars, and to cherish the goodness that each season brings.

It's a call to embrace the impermanence of life and find gratitude in myriad experiences. You can't fully appreciate the beauty without beholding the ugliness. I remind my children when we're stargazing in the backyard of our beautiful house that somewhere in the world at this very moment someone's enduring something so awful that we can't imagine it.

This journey has shifted my perspective. It's not about grand achievements or worldly conquests anymore. Instead of grasping, grasping, grasping, I've become intentional about finding joy in what's right in front of me. I set out each morning to soak up the beauty of life, to appreciate the mundane, to marvel at my luck in bearing witness to my beautiful surroundings. Being in the present is all we're here to do.

Ecstasy and agony are the black-and-white cookie of the human condition. They exist side by side. Unless you're content to nibble around the edges of life, you can't have one without the other. I want my children to take huge bites out of this one beautiful existence we've been gifted. I want them to know that they can trust people. They can love someone deeply without fear that they'll disappear. I also want them to be clear that even the most beautiful relationships contain ugly moments. They are going to get hurt, and that's okay. They'll be okay. It's up to me to give them the tools to mine all the richness from their one big, beautiful life. I'm doing my best to teach them to trust that God and the universe will work for and through them.

By the grace of God, I've gotten this far. I have a ways to go to get to where I need to be, to live from a place of *healed* and not *surviving*. I'll know I've gotten there when I can tell you who I aspire to be five years from now. What will my future self look like? I'm a mapmaker charting a new route, but as uncertain as that path may be, I do know this for sure: I'm the mother, sister, friend, coworker, and boss that I am because of everything I've experienced.

I'm not done. Hopefully not by a long shot. I've gotten this far through resilience, a lot of help from my friends, and dumb luck. The journey my children and I are on—that maybe you're on, too—is a marathon with no finish line in sight. All we can do is keep moving forward, step-by-step, and trust that when we stumble—because we *will* stumble—we can pick one another up.

The children and I, we could have gone all wobbly, but no. We're a four-legged step stool: sturdy and built to boost one another. Despite what we've gone through, we haven't lost sight of one another. As we say all the time, "We've got this because we've got one another."

ACKNOWLEDGMENTS

Writing this book has been a challenging journey, and it would not have been possible without the support of so many incredible people.

To my team, my chosen family—Julie, Sarah, Megan, Mike, Jared, Gail, Adrienne, Kat, Korinne, and Chaisten—thank you for your unwavering support, guidance, and love. Your encouragement made this labor of love possible.

To the Harper Horizon team, especially Matt, Meaghan, and Kevin—thank you for believing in this project from the beginning. And to Karen, for your time and care in bringing my story to life.

To the police department, NAMI, and Our House Grief Support Center—thank you for supporting my family when we needed it most.

To my dance family and fans—your continued support over the past two decades means the world to me.

To my friends—thank you for lifting me up and making life worth living.

To Connie and the Boss family—thank you for raising such a remarkable person in Stephen.

To my parents, David and Nikki, and siblings Dave, Aaron, Jessica, and Becky—your unconditional love is my greatest treasure.

Finally, to my children—Weslie, Maddox, and Zaia—I love you dearly, and we will keep dancing through life together.

NOTES

CHAPTER 5: STEPHEN

60 **"I might have been clashing helmets with you":** Lewis Howes, host, "Twitch Boss the Hip Hop Dancing Legend on Creating Success Your Way with Lewis Howes," *The School of Greatness*, podcast, November 13, 2016, YouTube, 1:15:02, https://youtu.be /2WFjtqCN8jQ?si=CVM1haWb8Cgu8p5N.

63 **"Love wins":** Stephen tWitch Boss (@sir_twitch_alot), "Love wins," Instagram, June 12, 2020, www.instagram.com/p/CBWhCPYjbRl.

63 **"I was able to marry the love of my life":** Allison Holker (@allisonholker), "I was able to marry the love of my life . . . ," Instagram, June 12, 2020, www.instagram.com/p/CBWuOQ4hORB.

CHAPTER 6: ONE AND ONLY

73 **"Well, I won't give up on us":** Jason Mraz, "I Won't Give Up," track 4 on *Love Is a Four Letter Word*, Atlantic Records, 2012, CD..

CHAPTER 7: PUSH IT REAL GOOD

90 **"Three, six, nine, damn she fine":** Lil John & The East Side Boyz, "Get Low," track 19 on *Kings of Crunk*, BME and TVT, 2002, CD.

90 **"(Push it) / Push it real good!":** Salt-N-Pepa, "Push It!" B-side on *Tramp*, Next Plateau Entertainment and London Recordings, 1987, 12″ record.

90   **"She can make angels'":** Stephen tWitch Boss (@sir_twitch_alot), "'She can make angels, I've seen it with my own eyes . . . ,'" Instagram, April 3, 2016, www.instagram.com/p/BDwZwaAQ6LW.

93   **"How long have you known and kept this from me?":** "tWitch & Allison's Big Announcement!," TheEllenShow, May 10, 2019, YouTube, 1:49, www.youtube.com/watch?v=QPDMHdjVQcc.

96   **"It's fun to have dance as a way for us to connect":** "tWitch & Allison Holker Boss Extended Interview," *The Jennifer Hudson Show*, December 17, 2022, YouTube, 6:54, www.youtube.com/watch?v=kZ81E4GvijY.

CHAPTER 8: THE BOSS FAMILY

102   **"Let's make it the best time in our lives":** Alicia Keys, "December Back 2 June," track 4 on *Santa Baby*, Alicia Keys Records, 2022, CD.

CHAPTER 9: BABY, ARE YOU OKAY?

105   **"tWitch, one last time, dance with me":** "tWitch's last dances on The Ellen Show with Ellen DeGeneres–farewell season," Ellen DeGeneres World, January 5, 2023, YouTube, 8:33, www.youtube.com/watch?v=dhg5luPIRZ4.

109   **"Be the first to give yourself some grace":** Stephen tWitch Boss (@sir_twitch_alot), "JULY 14, 2022 REMINDERS FOR LIFE," Instagram, July 14, 2022, www.instagram.com/p/CgADUyWLFoU.

113   **"You are always attracting the support and resources needed":** Stephen tWitch Boss (@sir_twitch_alot). "NOVEMBER 15, 2022 REMINDERS FOR LIFE," Instagram, November 15, 2022, www.instagram.com/p/Ck_GEuxLRC8.

CHAPTER 13: A STAGGERING DISCOVERY

152   **Stephen was one of 49,476 Americans to die by suicide:** "Facts About Suicide," Centers for Disease Control, National Center for Health Statistics, April 25, 2024, https://www.cdc.gov/suicide/facts/.

157   **"If I had to choose one thing":** Lewis Howes, host, "Twitch Boss the Hip Hop Dancing Legend on Creating Success Your Way," *The School of Greatness*, podcast, November 14, 2016, YouTube, 1:15:02, www.youtube.com/watch?v=2WFjtqCN8jQ.

160   **"One of the cutest couples on TikTok!":** "tWitch & Allison Holker Boss Extended Interview," *The Jennifer Hudson Show*, December 17, 2022, YouTube, 6:54, www.youtube.com/watch?v=kZ81E4GvijY.

CHAPTER 15: HOME SWEET HOME

187   **"A year of missing you":** Weslie Renae (@weslie.renae), "A year of missing you, but not a single day goes by without thinking of what you've given to the world," Instagram, December 13, 2023, www.instagram.com/p/C0zn9cPSLPr.

191   **Serenity Prayer:** "The Serenity Prayer and Twelve Step Recovery," Hazelden Betty Ford Foundation, October 14, 2018, www.hazeldenbettyford.org/articles/the-serenity-prayer.

192   **"Just because I don't wear dresses and bright pink":** Weslie Renae (@weslierenae83), TikTok, www.tiktok.com/@weslierenae83 (no longer available).

CHAPTER 16: FINDING MY VOICE

198   **"I want to take you back to a time in my life":** Emily Kirkpatrick, "Tyler Perry Reflects on His Own Suicide Attempts After DJ Stephen 'Twitch' Boss's Death," *Vanity Fair*, December 16, 2022, https://www.vanityfair.com/style/2022/12/tyler-perry-suicide-attempts -mental-health-depression-dj-twitch-stephen-boss-death. The video was posted to Perry's Instagram account (@tylerperry) at https://www.instagram.com/reel/CmKz8jEqCc but is no longer available.

201   **"I'm really, really inspired":** "Auditions: Day One," *So You Think You Can Dance*, Season 18, episode 1, aired March 4, 2024, on FOX.

ABOUT THE AUTHOR

ALLISON HOLKER first burst onto the scene when she competed in Season 2 of *So You Think You Can Dance*. Her skill and popularity led her to return as an All-Star on the show in Season 7, where she met fellow dancer Stephen "tWitch" Boss, whom she married in December 2013.

As an Emmy-nominated choreographer and on-air personality, Allison was last seen as a judge on *So You Think You Can Dance* and was featured as a professional dancer on *Dancing with the Stars*. She appeared in the first two seasons of VH1's scripted series *Hit the Floor* and performed in *A Chance to Dance*, *Make Your Move*, and *High School Musical*. She has served as cohost of *Disney's Fairy Tale Weddings*; E!'s *The Funny Dance Show*; and her own digital series *Dance Like a Boss*, alongside tWitch, which aired on EllenTube. She hosted HGTV's most popular competition series, *Design Star: Next Gen*, where talented designers, renovators, and social media brand builders compete in intense weekly challenges.

Allison is also the author of a children's book, *Keep Dancing Through*; an ambassador for NAMI, the National Alliance on Mental Illness; and the founder of the Move with Kindness Foundation.

Allison is a devoted mother to her three children, Weslie, Maddox, and Zaia.